WHAT'S HAPPENING TO HOME?

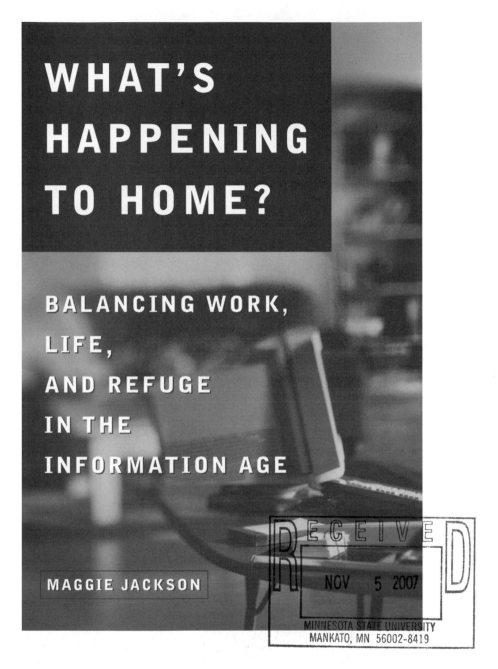

WHAT'S HAPPENING TO HOME?

BALANCING WORK, LIFE, AND REFUGE IN THE INFORMATION AGE

MAGGIE JACKSON

 SORIN BOOKS   Notre Dame, IN

Grateful acknowledgment is made for permission to reprint excerpts from the following publications:

The Domestication of the Human Species by Peter Wilson, published by Yale University Press, New Haven, 1988.

"Once More to the Lake," in *One Man's Meat* by E. B. White, published by Harper Brothers, New York, 1938. Reprinted by permission of Tilbury House, Gardiner, Maine.

© 2002 by Mπaggie Jackson

www.sorinbooks.com

International Standard Book Number: 1-893732-40-1

Cover by Angela Moody, Moving Images

Text design by Katherine Robinson Coleman

Printed and bound in the United States of America.

Library of Congress Cataloging-in-Publication Data
Jackson, Maggie.
What's happening to home? : balancing work, life, and refuge in the information age / Maggie Jackson.
 p. cm.
Includes bibliographical references.
ISBN 1-893732-40-1 (pbk.)
1. Employees--Effect of technological innovations on. 2. Work and family. I. Title.
HD6331 .J33 2002
306.3'6'0973--dc21

2001005238
CIP

For John

Contents

Acknowledgments

In writing this book, I've often been alone, but rarely lonely. Many people along the way gave me ample time and encouragement. Their support made my journey a shared adventure. Their interest made the work a pleasure, every step of the way.

My primary thanks must go to the more than 225 people I interviewed for this book. Some told me about their research and work. Many spoke freely about their own homes—their feelings, ideas, hopes, and daily struggles. I am grateful.

For research support, I would like to thank the New York Society Library, especially Susan Chan; the New York Public Library; Stuart Basefsky of the Catherwood Library, School of Industrial and Labor Relations at Cornell University; Leigh Gavin of the Chicago Historical Society; Claes Jernaeus of the Consulate General of Sweden; and Tricia Rosen of Greenfield Online. For technical help, I'm indebted to Dana Bloch, Ric Holzman, and Joe Little. Robert Burge was a white knight in real estate. I appreciate the grant given by the Sloan Foundation and the leave of absence extended by The Associated Press. I am deeply indebted to Ellen Galinsky and Katherine Davis in myriad ways.

Gabriella Augustsson, Deborah Burand, Stephanie Coontz, Jodi Kravitz, Chris Sullivan, and Peter Svensson astutely criticized early drafts. Lisa Brainerd, Irene Kunii, Frances Little, Wallis Miller, Cindy Wentworth Murphy, and Lise Strickler gave me sisterly encouragement. For their interest and support, I also want to thank my book club, and my extended family—Tante, Li, Carl, Jim, Ann Marie, Betty, Dave, Sally, Violy, and Jola.

Thank you, Jim Levine, Bob Hamma, and John Kirvan, for having faith in this book.

Most of all, thank you, John, Emma, and Anna for making our home.

Introduction

I never expected to write a book about home. I am a devoted urbanite who has lived on three continents in twenty years, not a homebody. I care little for matters of décor, and you won't catch me puttering around a garden or lovingly wielding a hammer or paintbrush in my house. I am not an architect, builder, or maven of the domestic arts. In a way, I stumbled upon the importance of home when I least expected to. The beginnings of a new vision of home came to me one spring in a sweet-smelling bedroom where two little girls in bunk beds were snuggling down to sleep.

My daughters often beg for bedtime stories, and I routinely oblige them with cuddles in the dark and tales of fairies and elves and brave children. They wiggle with delight under their blankets at happy endings, and howl with terror if the plot turns scary. We all love this time of day. But not too long ago, rather than linger, I found myself hurrying to give them their last sips of water, and if they were especially talkative, I'd snap, "Go to bed! Mommy has to finish her work!"

That gave me pause. I always had made it a priority to spend loads of time with them. Working after they slept seemed a guilt-free bargain. Yet here I was brandishing job deadlines over the quiet of their bedtime hour. They needed to get to bed, but something seemed terribly wrong.

At the time, I was working three days a week, but because my job as a workplace columnist demanded much more than that, I went to the office a fourth day and slipped in work at home nearly every evening. I was accustomed to working after hours. Before PCs, I read papers and books at night. On my first Apple computer, I tapped out articles after dinner. Finally, with the arrival of one laptop and two children, evenings revolved around work. After my daughters went to bed, I interviewed people ending their day in San Diego or Seattle.

I had set out to gain more flexibility, only to find myself scrambling to fit more work into my private life. No wonder I had this nagging feeling that things had gotten out of hand as I stood in my children's bedroom, urging them none-too-gently to get to sleep. During these rushed moments at the end of the day, I felt that the old rules of work were gone, but I was having trouble making up the new ones. Even more, my domestic life had changed dramatically, and I wondered what I'd gained and what I'd lost in the process. I had a hunch that if I kept on going this way, I wouldn't have much of a home life anymore.

I began to ask myself, what is a home in the twenty-first century? Today, our ways of work, marriage, and communication are so different from the past. Our definition of family has been transformed. What about our ideas of home? As we move from the Industrial Age to the computer era, shouldn't we reexamine the nature of this intimate corner of our lives? Amid my confusion, my eyes began to open to the importance of home.

Looking back at my work in the last few years, I noticed that my writing concerned home more than I had realized. I interviewed secretaries who toted laptops on vacation. I tracked a rise in home offices. I wrote about the growth in daycare centers and coffee bars at work. I was focusing on changes in people's jobs, yet questions about their lives outside work quietly surfaced each time. Two of my articles, in particular, made me realize that home should be a starting point for any discussion of balance, rather than an afterthought. Home should lie at the heart of our arguments about the role of technology in our lives, or the changing nature of family and community life.

In the 1990s, companies began to offer many new perks to their employees, partly because of the increasing shortage of talented workers. Along with daycare and health clubs, corporations set up dry cleaning, grocery stores, and even elementary schools at the office. Such benefits undoubtedly help many workers with their work-life balance. But what happens when people are exercising, getting check-ups, schooling their children, buying gifts, and working at their companies? Amenities may ebb and flow according to the health of the economy, but the trend is clear: the company, in effect, becomes a surrogate home. And looking for home at the office raises intricate questions about power and freedom. I made this point in an article that must have resonated with many, because it was published in more than 165 newspapers.

Certainly, there always will be what sociologist Christena E. Nippert-Eng calls "segmentors" who strive to separate work and home. My brother-in-law is one. Dave, an engineer, reads work papers during his sixty-minute train ride to and from his office, although he refuses to join the ranks of the commuters who jabber on cell phones all the trip. He'll stay late at his office to finish his work. But once Dave steps off the train in the evening, his work stops. He walks rain or shine, across a bridge, up a hill, and along a quiet wooded street, and he's home. No work calls, no overtime hours invade his weeknights or weekends. That way, he returns to work refreshed, he says.

But the pendulum is swinging the other way. Not only are people "home-ing" at work, but they are bringing their work back home, as farmers and craftsmen did for centuries. Zoologist Edward O. Wilson calls the trend "heartening and healthful" and a return to hunter-gatherer times. I set out to explore this course of events in an article examining work-life balance in the past century. Once again, a story I assumed concerned work wound up inspiring me to think about home.

To start, I interviewed more than sixty families across the country to find one that exemplified a century of changes in work-home balance. I found the Rovners, hardware store owners who had lived over the business, moved to the suburbs, and raised a son who often worked out of his home as a computer consultant. I went to Baltimore to interview Howard Rovner, whose father founded the business in the 1940s. Setting up my tape recorder in his neat kitchen, I naively expected him to reminisce about growing up over the store, seeing his dad for hours every day.

That wasn't what Howard Rovner told me. He'd seen his dad a lot, but as they worked. As a boy, he had little time for after-school play. Even on Sundays, customers would come knocking, asking his dad to sell them a mousetrap or a handful of nails. As soon as they could afford to, his parents bought a house in the suburbs in order to put distance between home and work. I learned a lot from the Rovners, and not least of my lessons was remembering to shed nostalgic assumptions before trying to learn from the past. Work can overpower home when these spheres are reconnected, if we're not careful.

Howard Rovner's high-tech son, however, forged a life akin to his grandfather's. When I visited Dave Rovner, he described using his cell phone on the golf course, taking his kids to work on Saturdays as he caught up on paperwork, and pulling out his laptop after they went to bed at night. He kept his work and home lives as closely fused as layers of a cake. But he was constantly questioning—as I was—whether he could turn off work after blending it with home. I told Dave jokingly about an executive who makes cell phone calls from chair lifts while on ski vacations. Every once in a while during the day I spent with Dave, he'd look at me and ask, "That's not as bad as the guy on the chair lift, is it?"

Like many of us, Dave Rovner was confused about how to handle the complexities of modern life: cell phones, laptops, longer work hours, the accelerating pace of each day. Yet he paid little attention to the role of home in this maelstrom.

Nor is he alone. I set out to write this book because I realized that I needed to pay more attention to home. After writing about the new company town, talking with Dave Rovner, hurrying my girls to bed so I could work—I began to understand that we all need to think again about home. Home isn't just the absence of work or an afterthought of life. Home shouldn't be snatched on the fly, between more "important" items on our agendas.

Nor should our homes be relics of the past. Think of the adages: "A man's house is his castle," or "Home Sweet Home." The words conjure up syrupy visions of aprons and lace, coziness and manners, lawn mowers and Betty Crocker—images that make me squeamish. Many aspects of our idea of home are outdated. A family is no longer only defined as a breadwinner, homemaker, and two children.

The American dream is no longer lived out in ranch houses in spanking new suburbs. A woman's place is no longer solely in the home.

The resonant power of these ideals, however, is one reason why many Americans aren't thinking anew about the meaning and culture of home. These traditions cast a shadow over the very word "home." Anyone, especially a woman, who wants to value home is easily accused of wanting to restore Victorian Age ideals. As I set out on the journey of writing this book, I repeatedly had to confront my own visceral unease with these visions of the past. Time and again, I was my own worst accuser, until I realized with certainty that we can update the idea of home.

We can construct a new vision of home, without shackling anyone to its framework. We can redefine home without shortchanging the work lives so many of us value. Men and women, single parents, single people, male breadwinners, working women, homemaker moms, the Internet Generation, aging Boomers—all need to think anew about home. I hope this book will help you begin doing that.

As you can guess by now, this is not a book about the history of domestic architecture or the art of interior decoration. If you want to build a summer house, learn how to furnish your home office, or plan a month of dinner menus, this is not the book for you.

But if you question how a computer in your bedroom may affect your private life, or if you wonder whether dividing your time between two houses will split or reunite your families, this book will prove useful. If you know you don't want to re-create your parents' home, but you aren't sure what you do want in a home, read on. If my words make you feel uneasy, curious, angry, or enlightened so far, I hope you will join me on this journey. You'll even learn about architecture, summer houses, and home economics— in so far as they shed light on the meaning and culture of home today.

Rather than hand you a "how-to," I hope to shatter your assumptions about this crucial part of our lives, then lead you on your own path toward creating a home in the twenty-first century. Again, I can't tell you exactly how to do this. There's no such thing as the "Ten Sure-Fire Rules for Creating Home." Between chapters, I include short excerpts from a diary I kept while writing this book. But I don't do so to offer myself as a model. These thoughts show how my home is a work-in-progress, blemishes and all. We each will make a different home, perhaps more so than at any other time in human history. This absence of rules is exciting but frightening. The idea of home is more subjective and personal than ever. But that's why home has the power to touch us so deeply. It is so uniquely ours.

Even so, we can share a language of home. Our homes vary by person, by era, and by culture, yet certain timeless qualities consistently remain integral to the idea of home. For instance, humans have long tried to craft homes that keep private life apart from the rough-and-tumble world. Different cultures and eras define "apart" and "private" in varying ways, yet in almost all societies, home serves as a place of both physical and psychological protection. In Mehinacu Indian villages in central Brazil, tribe members live in large, communal houses. Yet strict rules, such as respecting separate family areas within the open houses, protect villagers' domestic privacy. Home is also a starting point of our life, and a time and place where we can be ourselves.

In this new millennium, we are already changing the meaning of home, often unconsciously. In the first half of this book, I explore these changes. In the way we furnish and build our houses, we are embracing working at home in a way that, at first glance, seems to re-create the past. But in an era of ubiquitous computing, work can invade domestic life to a degree never experienced before. In making our homes permeable to the Internet and mobile technology, we also redefine the meaning of domestic privacy, creating a marketplace for this once-valued right. Finally, we are hiring outsiders to manage all aspects of our domestic life, a trend that raises questions about the role of caring in a home.

These trends blur the lines between work and home, public and private—turning our homes into bustling centers of work and communications. This idea of home is flexible and individualistic. But in nurturing these changes, we risk losing our homes as refuges. I explore ways to preserve intimacy, quiet, and caring at home without returning to the rigid ideals of the past. By rebuilding some boundaries, we can create the sanctuaries we desperately need today.

The second half of the book examines how we are searching for "home" outside our homes. It is not just the new company town that serves as a surrogate home in this mobile age. Increasingly, we are speaking of "living in" our cars, treating them as home offices, entertainment centers, and movable dining spots. We seek home-like hotel rooms, and a growing segment of Americans divide themselves— with the help of technology—between two homes. In an age when time and place matter less and less, this trend can lead to a rootless diluting of the importance of home, or to a more mobile idea of domestic refuge. I hope to inspire you to catch hold of home, to keep it from slipping through your fingers, while redefining home to fit a mobile age.

As I kiss my daughters goodnight, open my laptop, and soul-search about home, I know I'm not alone. During nearly two years of travel and research, I've been amazed by people's reactions to this book. Mostly, they are surprised, then fascinated by this new approach to a very old subject. Amid the chaos of the nursery-school fall picnic, an ambitious young lawyer in a pinstriped suit puts down his paper plate and questions me, listening carefully to all I say about the changing meaning of home. A department store clerk, helping me buy a doll for my daughter's birthday, paused in a swirling sea of Christmas shoppers to quiz me on my research. On airplanes, at conferences, in schools, on vacation, people's wide-eyed looks and probing questions reveal to me a deep, often unrecognized hunger for rethinking the idea of home.

In writing this book, I've learned that home is not just an absence of work. It's not merely a moment of relaxation, grabbed wherever and whenever we can in the world. It's certainly not a matching set of furniture or the largest roof possible over our heads. A vision of home might include a quiet moment or a special chair. But home means more. It is a refuge for our humanity, a time and place intentionally crafted moment by moment.

I don't want to turn back the clock, to re-create the homes of ages past. Neither do I want to see crucial aspects of the refuge of home disappear in this new era. Without a refuge, we cannot find shelter from the world. Without shelter, we lose our best chances for intimacy, quiet, and privacy. Without a home, we're hardly human.

PART ONE:

THE
LOSSES
OF
HOME

The Architecture of Home-Work:

From Computer Armoires to Digital Walls

The things that surround us are inseparable from who we are.

Mihaly Csikszentmihalyi and Eugene Rochberg-Halton, *The Meaning of Things*

Enter the New York City apartment of Bill Lipschutz and Lynnelle Jones, and first you'll notice the sleek, stark rooms. Granite counters, slate floors, a stainless steel staircase—this is not a cozy, traditional home.

Step closer and you'll see the digital monitors. One hangs upside down and inverted in the bathroom, so Lipschutz can watch while shaving in the morning. Others beam out from the wall next to a curvy bathtub, and from a bedside cabinet. Stretching out for a nap, Lipschutz can lift a pillow and peek at another, set in the arm of a sofa. Altogether, nearly a dozen monitors peer out from the walls and furniture of this 1,500-square-foot space.

Lipschutz is a currency trader, placing bets on the daily rise and fall of monies worldwide. To stay abreast of the fluctuating Japanese yen or French franc, he tracks foreign markets that gyrate as most of America sleeps. This can mean keeping alert to the markets twenty-four hours a day, seven days a week, even while bathing, resting, and eating.

The apartment was built in 1988 when Lipschutz headed the foreign exchange desk at a major investment bank. He's now in business for himself, as is Jones, a former bond trader. Yet more than a decade after its creation, their home is still attracting attention—a segment by CNN, coverage in *Vogue* and major architectural journals, inclusion in an exhibit in The Museum of Modern Art in New York. The architecture is admired. But the apartment makes a splash for a quite different reason.

The very bones of the apartment enable the fusion of home and work—a goal that Americans increasingly share.

Architects Frank Lupo and Daniel Rowen, on instructions from Lipschutz, designed a space where the owners can switch deftly between work and home by the minute. Lipschutz's home office isn't grafted onto a third bedroom or poised on a dining room table that's swept clean for Sunday dinners. The apartment centers around a "trading room" that Lipschutz speaks of reverently. "I often trade all night long," he says. "So this is the perfect place for me to operate in a kind of trading cocoon without being disturbed by another person. This is a home office taken to a level that it couldn't have been taken to ten years ago." The ubiquitous monitors effectively allow him to work in every inch of his home. The very bones of the apartment enable the fusion of home and work—a goal that Americans increasingly share. Created at the dawn of the Internet Age, the apartment is a vision of our future.

Certainly, the average American family isn't likely to be shopping soon for stainless steel staircases. The Lipschutz/Jones apartment's spareness, its costly materials, are for the few. But that's just packaging. In the way we furnish, build, and use our homes, we're turning closer and closer toward Lipschutz's original goal. Today, some of the hottest-selling home furniture is designed to bring work into all parts of the house. Technologies that are no more than a few decades away from store shelves will allow work to permeate almost any object: our clothes, our walls, our kitchen counters. Cozy rooms are giving way to loft-like spaces.

Does this matter? After all, the look of a home is not its most important quality. Sleek and modern or cozy and worn, the architecture and furnishings of a house are not the end point to understanding home. But if we are to rethink the idea of home, we cannot ignore the tangible. How we build and design our homes speaks volumes about our identity and values. When we turn our dining room tables into workstations or tap into e-mail in the bedroom, we change our relationship to home. As I saw in my own evening gravitation toward my laptop, the domestic realm becomes a workplace all too easily. The pull of work accelerates the tempo of home. The push of the outside world competes with domestic priorities. We may never live in an apartment dotted with digital monitors, but many of us can already feel this push and pull. And the technological revolutions soon to come will hasten this transformation, raising crucial questions about the future of home.

In a job-centric culture, how can we reunite work and home, without losing sight of home? How can we preserve a domestic refuge without turning home back into a rigidly separate sphere? Is a sense of place important anymore in an increasingly virtual world? To begin to look for answers, we must reconsider how we're changing our houses and what the future may bring. This is our entryway to rebuilding home. This is the front door to a new vision of home.

Way down in Martinsville, Virginia, furniture maker Hank Long is pondering visions of the future. He's never heard of the Lipschutz/Jones apartment and doesn't much look to The Museum of Modern Art for inspiration. But as a top executive at Hooker Furniture, which stocks Main Street stores nationwide, Long sees the impact of the work-at-home movement on our lives. Our home offices are spilling into every corner of our houses.

Is a sense of place important anymore in an increasingly virtual world?

Hooker Furniture has introduced a line of home office furniture called "La Cocoon" designed by futurist Faith Popcorn. The computer cabinet, attached bookcase, and desk are done in a French country style, stained in either dark cherry or buttermilk. Each set features curtain panels over the desk that owners can match to their home decor. "It can even go in the kitchen," points out Long. The desks sport built-in flower vases and finished tops, so people won't see rough wood when looking down a staircase at a home office in the living room. Faith Popcorn is domesticating—and feminizing—the cubicle.

Furniture makers are selling home office pieces almost as quickly as they can make them. It's the fastest growing business segment for Hooker's competitor, Stanley Furniture. The company's revenues in this area would have doubled for a second consecutive year in 1999, except the Stanleytown, Virginia manufacturer couldn't keep up with demand. To take advantage of the market, Stanley opened a factory devoted to home office furniture in early 2000.

Yet most furniture makers are just beginning to catch up on the fact that home office equipment isn't being used just in the home office. People are toting their work from bedroom to kitchen, perching almost anywhere to peck on computers. Studies show that a majority of home offices are in multi-functional rooms: bedrooms, dens, dining rooms, living rooms, and kitchens. People even work in bathrooms. Hank Long himself knows a bit about such spillover. He recently moved into a house equipped with two offices, one in the family recreation room and the other in a bedroom. But he found both so noisy and inconvenient that he's just set up a desk in another room so he can "get some peace and quiet at night."

As office furnishings break out of the back bedroom, they're becoming items of decor. People want to work almost anywhere, but they also want the accoutrements of work to blend into home, perhaps to soften the lines between the two. "For e-mailing in bed, make sure your night table drawer is deep enough to store your laptop and wires," the editors of *House & Garden* confide. An article titled "Laptop of Luxury" shows a photo of a skinny laptop perched upon a woman's black vanity, surrounded by a silk purse, perfume bottles, a vase of lush yellow roses, and a jauntily thrown string of pearls. The home office as boudoir?

Minimalist design guru Philippe Starck's "Lazy Working Sofa" for Cassina helps bring computer work into the living room; it can be ordered with side and back tables replete with electrical outlets and a phone jack. Architectural designer Mary Douglas Drysdale predicts a comeback for "swing armchairs," the chairs with little attached desktops used in classrooms. But the most popular home office fashion item is the computer armoire, a resurrection of the large chests and cupboards used in homes before built-in closets became standard in the early nineteenth century. It's interesting that two hundred years later, we're re-adopting a symbol of domestic portability, this time for our work.

My neighbors acquired two computer armoires as they experimented with ways to import work into their home. At the time, she was telecommuting full-time, and he was bringing loads of work home. First, they set up computer armoires in separate parts of their apartment—a corner of the living room for him, a dining room niche for her. A year later, they hauled his workspace into the dining room, rewired telephone lines, added bookshelves, and turned the room into a shared office. To make the changes, they had to take leaves out of their dining room table, which soon became piled with paperwork. My husband and I wondered whether we'd be invited for dinner again.

Luckily we have, and when their armoires are shut and the paperwork is cleared, the room mostly looks like a dining room. Sometimes I envy their decision to make the leap and convert a space into a work area, rather than hiding bits and pieces of work around the apartment, as I do. Yet I also wonder whether they have a dining room anymore. Have they traded an under-used dining room they sometimes worked in for a well-used workroom that they sometimes dine in? The new home office furniture blends in so well and is so flexible that it's easy to forget the repercussions of bringing work into a room.

Perhaps because my husband and I don't work at home full-time we haven't considered transforming our dining room into an office. Even when I write there until midnight, I find myself removing every bit of paper and technology from the room before I sleep. We don't entertain any more than the average parents of young children—in other words, rarely. As a family, we eat most meals in our kitchen. Still, we relish having a dining room. To me, the sanctity of this space symbolizes our commitment to having one spot where human relations, not work worries, predominate. Is this an unattainable goal?

Computing belongs in furniture and footware much more than it does on the desktop.

MIT Media Lab

In coming decades, we won't worry about hiding computers in armoires or which sofa has the laptop plug. Closets and clothing, eyeglasses and kitchen counters, all will be computers. At home, people will work or surf wherever they're sitting, walking, or eating. The coming technology has enormous implications for the nature of home. The next generations of computers will enable us to alternate between work and home by the nanosecond, in every room of the house. I set out one fall day to visit a place where I might catch a glimpse of home's fate in this ultra-wireless world.

Tucked in a corner of the Massachusetts Institute of Technology's patchwork campus in greater Boston is a laboratory where hundreds of physicists, computer scientists, artists, and thinkers are trying to liberate the computer from its desktop box. MIT Media Laboratory researchers want to make computers an "invisible" yet highly responsive part of life. In this sense, invisible means blended into everyday objects, thus in a sense unseen. "Invisibility is the missing goal in computing," writes Media Lab Professor Neil Gershenfeld in his book *When Things Start to Think*.

At the Lab, which looks like a cross between a sleek science facility and a crazy toy shop, researchers are developing a book that can show any published work, yet is made of paper. The pages are covered with microencapsulated particles and electrodes, while the binding holds the electronics. "Pages other than the one you're looking at can be changing, so that all of *War and Peace* could be read in a pamphlet of just a few pages," writes Gershenfeld. Another project, a responsive shoe, picks up the news or a message from the boss as the wearer steps in his front door. Some of the Lab's researchers are already "cyborgs," wearers of portable computer equipment, nearly twenty-four hours a day.

Bill Buxton, a professor at the University of Toronto, offers a way to understand what's coming. In his writings, he compares the computer's evolution to historic changes in the way humans have kept warm. In early times, domestic architecture was driven by the paramount need to contain heat. An open fire offered little warmth, so caves were sought. Buxton compares this to the era when computers were so enormous that entire buildings had to be devoted to them.

Just as houses came to be built with fireplaces that provided warmth in one room, so a variety of buildings eventually housed computers, but only in special computer rooms. Next, radiators and Franklin stoves piped heat from room to room. That's akin to today's technology, which is available in any space that has the right "plumbing" or wiring. Finally, climate control systems allowed invisible delivery of heat—the kind of revolution that scientists now seek for computers.

> *There will be no difference between public and private, and work and home in future.*
>
> Kelly Heaton

Kelly Heaton, an MIT researcher in purple overalls and clogs, sits in a corner of the Lab one afternoon, fiddling with a colorful chain of magnetic cubes that looks like an unfolded Rubik's Cube. Each computerized cube can turn 256 colors, and project infinite graphics, such as traffic flow patterns or virtual pets. A big office supply company is interested in their future as mini-message centers that workers can shape and color as they wish. It's akin to an e-mail system you could tote in your pocket.

Downstairs at the Lab's "Kitchen of the Future," the linoleum is scuffed and countertops are a dull gray Formica, despite Martha Stewart's involvement as a consultant on the project. The room's unimpressive decor, however, belies its capabilities. A recipe for "Sour Cream Berry Tarts" beams onto the countertop. I touch a photo-icon of graham crackers and a computer voice pertly tells me how to start cooking. Tackling a recipe this way certainly lacks the tactile comfort of flipping open a well-worn *Joy of Cooking,* but it seems fast. Just as easily, the kitchen technology could display a work presentation on the counter, so you could catch up with e-mail while the tarts bake. An electronic tablecloth under development could bring Grandma online at Thanksgiving, or give a telecommuter the chance to hold a virtual meeting from home.

"There will be no difference between public and private, and work and home in future," says Heaton, whose workspace brims with screwdrivers, computer parts, and curios like Barbie dolls strung from the ceiling. "It's which information you invite into your personal space that determines the character of your environment."

Heaton confides that she deliberately doesn't own a cell phone. "A lot of people around here think that's archaic," she says. But she believes that even if a cell phone is turned off, just having one changes the perimeters of her accessibility to work. "You import office into your personal space, if you own one," she says briskly.

Nearby, Professor Judith Donath is pecking at a laptop in a spare office with no desktop computer in sight. A slim woman with celestial blue eyes and a ponytail, she agrees that in a world where work and home lives are fast blending, conscious decisions must be made about which technology is used at what time. In her fully wireless home, she and her husband—an Internet entrepreneur—can work anywhere, but try to do so in the same room so they can be together. If her toddler dawdles over his breakfast, she opens her laptop and works while he munches. In her view, that's no more unsociable than reading the newspaper in front of her child. To me, breaking away from a machine— where tasks must be completed or perhaps lost—seems harder than turning to and from a newspaper. However,

Donath's point, that we must weigh carefully the options technology gives us, is all too true.

I am visiting Donath because she's one of the few people at the Media Lab whose work is concerned with the human relations behind the technological gizmos. She leads the Sociable Media Group, which studies and maps relationships in the virtual community. In a sense, she's trying to give flesh and bone to chat rooms, speaker phone conversations, and other innovations that currently produce murky communications compared to in-person relations. She's trying to make virtual ties more visible, even as computers grow more invisible. Donath's work, for example, could lessen the "remote" qualities of telework, making virtual conversations and video-conferencing more realistic. If computer armoires help bring work into all rooms of the house, and tomorrow's computers bring work to all objects in the home, then Donath's projects bring the work community—clients, bosses, suppliers—into all parts of our homes.

Will there be any room for home in future houses?

One of Donath's projects, for example, shows who is logged on within a virtual community. She came up with the idea for the "Visual Who" while working in Japan. Feeling isolated from her colleagues at the Media Lab, she often found herself hunting through the computer to see who was online, hence available for a chat. In the working world, Visual Who would allow managers and employees to see instantly which home-workers are logged in, and vice versa. The system brings "face-time" (time spent in the office) right into the home. "If I'm online at three o'clock in the morning on a Saturday, I want people to know!" grins Donath.

I begin to wonder if there will be any room for home in future houses. Moving a computer armoire into your dining room might spell the decline of family suppers. But ubiquitous computing could eclipse time for home anywhere in your house. Will we beam berry tart recipes on our counters, or just hurriedly check e-mail during breakfast? Will we control this pervasive technology, or will our shoes and tables, along with our pagers and cell phones, beep and ring at us during dinner?

Consider for a moment preindustrial times, when most people—blacksmiths, farmers, doctors, millers—worked in their homes. Work was often constant and, at least in medieval times, took place within the same physical spaces as sleep, eating, and pleasure. Still, boundaries existed between segments of life. The natural rhythms of sun and season, along with religious dictates, gave people shared cues to rest—temporal borders that strongly divided home and work. By the seventeenth century, some urban builders, lawyers, and civil servants in Europe worked in offices, while those who still toiled at home did so in rooms more explicitly set aside for crafts or trades. Life's borders may have been flexible and ever-changing, but they firmly existed.

More than ever before, today's technology has the potential to erase nearly all boundaries between home and work, public and private. Ubiquitous computing makes home permeable to an accelerating world, a world where the anchors of time and place matter less and less. In this new all-in-one world, we risk losing a time and place for home.

And such an era is not far off. Many of the innovations being created at the Media Lab are just decades away from showing up at your neighborhood Radio Shack. The Lab's 170 sponsors, ranging from Lego to the U.S. Postal Service, are bringing these projects both to the consumer market and their own workplaces. Then people will adopt them, judging by the public appetite for technology. Just look at the growing popularity of networked homes, which allow for fast Internet connections and the sharing of data and printers between computers. When IBM paired with a Houston developer to build one of the country's first communities with networked homes, twenty-three were sold in their first two weeks on the market—quadruple the rate of sales at traditional developments.

Architect Gisue Hariri has faith in the growth of such markets. She and her sister and partner, Mojgan, hope to build a house that carries the idea of networked countertops to a whole other level, and they have serious interest from two prospective clients. Like the inventions of the Media Lab, the Hariris' Digital House provides a peek into a future that is closer than we think. Only this time, the idea isn't just to infuse our furniture with computers, it's to make the house itself a veritable PC.

Gisue Hariri makes two cups of strong tea one autumn day in her Manhattan studio and introduces me to the Digital House. Speaking in the lilting accent of her native Iran, she passionately describes how the sisters plan to use computer screens as the very fabric of the structure. "We tried to use the technology as a building block, that's why I find it potent and exciting," she says. "I want one of those houses!" In the Digital House, the walls and windows will be made from liquid crystal display screens, the sort found on laptops. When turned on, they will act as computer or video monitors. When shut off, they become transparent, floor-to-ceiling windows and doors. One computer-generated picture of the house shows a life-sized virtual chef beaming on the wall behind the kitchen stove, ready to assist a lithe woman in an evening dress with a recipe flashed beside him. My thoughts drift to a different picture: my editor beaming himself into my kitchen during breakfast, barking that the staff meeting will be displayed on my dining room wall at 8 a.m. sharp, ready or not.

The Digital House even looks like a glass and steel laptop standing on end, with boxes glued on the sides. Its thin, rectangular core (the laptop) is expanded with prefab rooms (the boxes), added where owners choose to place them. It's another sign that the era of mucking about with computer armoires in dining rooms is transitional as we move into the Information Age. In the Digital House, you can add a workspace wherever you like, long after you've built the core structure.

Today's technology has the potential to erase nearly all boundaries.

This flexibility, along with ubiquitous technology, could be seen again and again in "The Un-Private House," The

Museum of Modern Art exhibit that featured both the Lipschutz/Jones apartment and the Digital House, along with twenty-four other houses and planned homes. Curator Terence Riley put together the exhibit to illustrate how homes are evolving due to the changing nature of family, private life, and work. In the accompanying catalog, Riley discusses trends such as the reintroduction of work into the home, the permeability of houses to "images, sounds, text, and data," the growth of one-person households. For Riley, the exhibition's houses are both a "collective bellwether" of his field and a harbinger of the future.

It's difficult to see the link between these sleek, modern houses and the average American home, present or future. Those in the exhibit are more reminiscent of the glass boxes made famous by early twentieth-century architect Mies van der Rohe than the average American home. One traditionalist architect, upon hearing that I was interviewing participants in "The Un-Private House" exhibit, turned apoplectic. "That's just a bunch of masturbating artists! That's not real life," he yelled.

Yet just as Lipschutz's monitors foreshadow the push to bring home offices into all corners of the house and the Media Lab's inventions give a taste of pervasive technology to come, so "The Un-Private House" exhibit hints at how our homes will evolve. We may never dwell in as sci-fi a home as the Digital House, but we have a very good chance of soon winding up with a video-conferencing wall in our dining room or a couch with a laptop jack. Few people wear *haute couture*, but elements of these designs trickle down to stores all over America, influencing Main Street attire every day.

Already, along with snapping up furniture designed to blend home and work, we're designing houses with fluid spaces reminiscent of Bill Lipschutz's apartment. One builder's house features an upstairs hallway with a wall that can be removed to make an open play area. Formal living rooms are shrinking, while family rooms combined with kitchens are burgeoning. Such "great rooms" hearken back to medieval times, when bourgeois houses centered on a large hall where families, servants, apprentices, and friends ate, slept, cooked, worked, and entertained. These trends again beg the question: When the bones of a house are constructed to allow work and home, or outside and inside, to reunite, how can we keep our home as a refuge? In Los Angeles, architects Danelle Guthrie and Tom Buresh, a married couple with a son, set out a few years ago to find out just that.

> *We're in a curious place of being both a scientist and being in a scientific experiment.*
>
> Danelle Guthrie

The experiment is the WorkHouse, the home Guthrie and Buresh built for themselves in 1996. Unlike the Digital House, which is still on the drawing board, and unlike the "Kitchen of the Future," which is a laboratory model, the WorkHouse has been tested and tried, experienced and occupied. It's a home, not just four walls with things inside; and like the Lipschutz apartment, the WorkHouse was deliberately designed to bring together work and home lives. In this sense, the experience of Guthrie and Buresh may teach us about our future as we embrace the idea of working in all parts of our homes.

The couple wasn't living far from their architecture business when they began yearning for change. The two miles that separated home and work constantly forced them to choose between being on the job or being at home. Danelle Guthrie felt particularly torn after the birth of their son in 1988, since then she could only work when her son was in daycare. She wanted to be home for him, but missed having a high degree of participation in the business that she and her husband had started together. The answer seemed to be to try and reconcile the physical division that existed between their home and work.

Yet the couple wanted to do more than graft their work onto a traditional home. Early on, they wrestled with the questions many of us are beginning to ask today as we work in the domestic realm. Is the dining room a place for family meals, or an extension of the office? If we buy furniture that allows it to be both, how do we manage to switch from one activity to the other without diluting the importance of either? Guthrie and Buresh wanted to build a house in which both the activities of home and work were valued. They didn't want a work studio in a back bedroom, where clients might see their dirty laundry. Nor did they want work to eclipse family life. "We really struggled with the idea of making a house feel like a house and making an office be an office, and yet merging them," Danelle tells me in a long telephone chat one Sunday afternoon.

One evening a few months later, I'm navigating the winding streets of West Hollywood, excited at the chance to visit the WorkHouse. In the darkness, at first I see only the house's spare, boxy outline. But when I enter, I'm enveloped in a warm, golden light. Nearly the entire interior is swathed in honey-colored plywood, patterned with the swirl of the wood grain. It's the only modernist house I've seen that could be called homey. Tom is meeting with a client, so Danelle pours a glass of wine, sits with her dog at her feet, and continues her story. A sandy-haired woman with an earthy face, she speaks in a crackling voice and laughs easily.

The three-level WorkHouse is almost entirely open, save for bathrooms and their son Ryan's bedroom. All other spaces, including the master bedroom, flow into one another, connected by a staircase. To shield the work area from the domestic spaces, the architects cloistered their studio on the second floor. That way, clients and employees could barely glimpse the living areas as they passed up the stairs from the front door to the office. The goal was to keep a professional separation between home and work, while creating easy transitions between the two. No door, no hallway, no two-mile commute separated work and home in the WorkHouse.

I couldn't stand having people in the house seven days a week.

Danelle Guthrie

As time went by, however, Danelle and her husband realized the drawbacks of living in a blended space. On a typical day, Ryan left for school and their employees arrived, making their morning coffee in the kitchen, before heading upstairs to the office. If a meeting was scheduled, the dining area served as the conference center. In mid-afternoon, Ryan returned, poking his head into the refrigerator and yelling upstairs, "Mom, do we have any snacks?" as his mom tried to finish talking to a client on the telephone.

"My attention was diverted and distracted, solving that problem, or trying to get homework done," Danelle says. "To make matters worse, often the people who work for us would have to stay past 6 p.m. and I'd be making dinner while they were upstairs. We avoided doing work on the weekends because I couldn't stand having people in the house seven days a week." Her voice still grinds with tension at the memory.

The day after my first visit, I return in the morning. Ryan is at school, Tom is giving a lecture, and the house is quiet as Danelle and I sit in the sunlit second-floor architecture studio—now in the midst of being converted to a family room. Bookshelves are being dismantled, only one computer remains. Just before The Museum of Modern Art featured the WorkHouse in its "Un-Private House" exhibit as a "revitalization of the residence/office model," the architects moved their studio out to a small cottage at the front of their property. The timing of the change is painfully ironic to Danelle Guthrie. She and her husband were questioning the premise of their inclusion in the show, even as it opened in New York.

Living and working in the WorkHouse taught Danelle that her family needed to redraw the boundaries between work and home. "When I would go home in Ryan's younger years, it really would be home," she said. "Now, the outside world, which is the work world, is constantly pulling at us. We have so little time that we spend together." These days, when she leaves the studio-cottage, crosses the driveway, and goes home, she rarely takes work phone calls, and she asks her staff to save questions for the morning, so she is available for her son after school. Essentially, she and her husband restored the commute they had left behind. "I've never been able to function well in a completely open office," admits Danelle. "I have to have some degree of separation."

Recovering their home life has not been easy. Even after taking the studio out, Danelle found that she had trouble relaxing in the WorkHouse, which had become nearly synonymous with work. But she and her husband have found, through trial and error, ways to preserve home. She finds the WorkHouse garden a place of repose. Just after my visit, she and her husband, for the first time, stayed home for a weekend of pure rest.

A home isn't just a house. Watch a child endlessly configure the furniture in a dollhouse. He expresses his idea of home each time he moves the television to center-stage in the living room, or decides who shares a bedroom. So, too, in grown-up houses, the placement of our furniture and walls is a starting point, a front door perhaps, to understanding the changing nature of home. Even as seemingly small a gesture as placing a computer armoire in the dining room has repercussions that we don't at first see. More exotic architectural visions of home, such as the Digital House or the Lipschutz apartment, foreshadow an era of blurred boundaries and ubiquitous technology. Unless we stop and carefully consider such changes, we eventually may wake up in a home without sanctuary, a home exposed to the world.

In building the WorkHouse, Danelle Guthrie and Tom Buresh gained the ability to move quickly and easily between their work and home lives. Yet these two parts of their lives deteriorated into a confusing jumble, inspiring them to restore some separation between them. In my own life, I'm still struggling to find the right balance between work and home at home. But instinctively I've drawn a line around my dining room, trying to preserve this space as a place separate from work. In a sense, I'm learning that a place for home must be consciously set aside. A sense of place does have a role to play in the creation of home.

The blending of work and home also raises questions of whether privacy can still exist in a domestic space shared by work. Can a feeling of repose be found in a house shared by such a public activity? Can we relax once we invite the world inside? "Domestic life, I think, requires some privacy," muses Danelle Guthrie. "When one always feels that one's publicly being viewed, it's hard to get clarity or deal with things that are very personal and sometimes messy and problematic." Privacy is the emotional wall encircling a home, and a further key to understanding the role of time and place in today's domestic life.

As for Bill Lipschutz, he's made changes in the years he's owned his New York apartment. He and his wife bought a house in Connecticut, where they now live. In the city, Lipschutz has moved his main trading desk out to the dining area. The old trading room has been turned into a library. The apartment is essentially an office, where he sleeps on many weeknights. In his mélange of work and home, few vestiges of home remain.

Diary: Room-to-Room Nomad

When I was a graduate student, I leaped headlong into academic life, studying almost continuously from September until June—and wearing myself out. Instead of relishing the wonderful detective work of my research, I was haunted by the feeling that another book should be read, another fact memorized. I didn't savor the learning, but gobbled up information thoughtlessly like a glutton. Although I did well in school, I paid a high price: losing the boundaries of my life. Now, facing a similarly boundary-less work—researching and writing a book—I panic. Well into my career, I've already lost my nights to work. I don't want to lose my chance to ever relax.

So before I leave my job for this project, I spend hours looking for an office—a spare bedroom, a corporate cubicle, any place I can call my own, work quietly, and use a telephone. I place ads, call business contacts, spread the word. As I struggle, I begin to look upon my little desk in the noisy newsroom as a bit of heaven; it is mine, it is just used for work, and it is "free"—in exchange for a day's toil, of course.

By the time my leave of absence rolls around, I have several possibilities:

▸ My bedroom. Easily sealed off from sounds of the house, the room is quiet. Still, I instinctively want to keep this place as a refuge from work. Moreover, my husband is an early bird, so late-night work sessions would be difficult.

▸ A small library. This workspace, twenty minutes from home, is nearly silent and has a scent akin to literary perfume. But without the use of a telephone, the space is impossible for interviews.

▸ A spare room in a friend's antiques business. Blissfully roomy, the office even has a door. However, it's forty-five minutes and two bus rides from my house, and lacks Internet access.

▸ My dining room table, where I've written articles in the quiet of the evening. I'm loathe, however, to sacrifice this place of family suppers and dinners with friends to the demands of work.

With this in mind, I begin.

One Sunday afternoon, I interview an architect, she at her home in California, I in my dining room in New York. John tries to keep the children away from me, but as the architect and I talk, my three-year-old enters the room four times, each time quietly whispering, "When will you finish?" On her face are big melt-your-heart grins. I gently keep shooing her away. As I conduct the interview, I smell dinner cooking, hear a bath filling for the children. I listen to the architect discuss her efforts to creatively design a home where work and rest can coexist, and I keep half an ear cocked for sounds of sibling fights.

The architect and I talk for an hour and fifteen minutes—too long for a Sunday evening work call, too short a time to delve deeply into our discussion.

The same night, I move most of my work materials into our newly painted bedroom, setting up shop on a long pine table my father built. Here, I can close the door when the little ones come home from school, and I can use a home phone, as well as my cell phone. I try to repress my visceral unease at using my bedroom as a home office. Gingerly, I begin trying out this new workspace, with its new chair, new angles of sunlight, new sounds. Are the extension cords for the telephone and computer lines long enough, I wonder?

T W O

Private Lives:
Making Time for Home
in a Connected World

Privacy is no longer drawn at the property line.

Terence Riley

Colin Ochel doesn't give clients his home number and wishes he hadn't divulged it at work. He won't read work e-mails on weekends and waited a year before installing a computer at home—although he's in the computer business. "I really wanted it as my sanctuary," the sandy-haired twenty-six-year-old says of his New York apartment, his first real home as an adult. "I think of it as that."

Ochel has built a private fiefdom behind symbolic walls, because for two years he lived an entirely public life. He sits one day, looking like a young man unaccustomed to wearing a suit, at a plastic conference table in the industrial loft where he and his partner Jeff Linnell built their computer animation business—and lived. For two years, they slept, ate, partied, and showered in the 4,000-square-foot space where they also worked endless hours. They each occupied one of seven freestanding wooden "pods" they'd had built in the huge space. That way, they could cut down on their expenses by both living and working there, and renting out the extra pods to students. It was a stroke of entrepreneurial ingenuity.

Within eighteen months, the experiment had soured. Ochel grew to despise the pods, and within two years, he had moved to the apartment he calls his sanctuary. "I really feel like I do have a kind of home," says Ochel. "I didn't have a home before at all." Linnell retreated to a small attic space—dubbed the cave—within the loft, accessible only by an enormous staircase on wheels, the kind you'd mount to board an airplane out on the tarmac. But he's also looking to find a home. "I want it to be everything that this place is not," says Linnell, a friendly, dark-haired young man with fatigue etched on his face. As I speak to them, the empty pods loom behind us, like barnacles stuck eerily inside a ship's hold. The student-tenants are long gone.

What went wrong? Certainly, it drove Ochel and Linnell crazy that they couldn't escape work. Ochel recalls that if he stepped out for a bite to eat, when he returned he couldn't help but see work. "So, you can't really remove yourself," he says. Furthermore, they had virtually no privacy. Friends joked that the space reminded them of *The Real World*, the MTV program that documents a group of strangers thrown together for months without escape.

The loft was intimate, too intimate. The walls of the twelve by twelve pods were insulated, but the sounds of conversations, music, and lovemaking wafted from the pods' paper roofs. If Linnell slept in after an all-nighter, he'd have to emerge awkwardly from his pod at mid-morning in front of his toiling staff. The students, who each stayed about six months, were encouraged to absent themselves during the day. Yet on more than one occasion, their private lives would clash with the public face of the business, as Linnell breathlessly described to me. "It's, like, 3 o'clock in the morning and you've got a client sitting there because he's there and he needs this thing now, and you've got six NYU students that just walked into a room and who knows what's going on in there. There's loud music and it's, you know, terribly distracting and a little embarrassing as well."

Even mundane domestic chores—the tiny repetitions that make up the fabric of private life—created tensions. Students got upset when Linnell, immersed in a project and working round the clock, wouldn't take a turn buying toilet paper or washing the breakfast dishes. "This is another arrogant and terrible way to look at things, but the fact of the matter was that I had my primary concern for the company and that's all!" says Linnell, fidgeting restlessly as he remembers those days. "People don't realize, people don't have the same perspective on it as when it's your company and your place and your home. They get confused by it."

And it was confusing. The students, attracted by a relative real estate bargain and perhaps by the exotic nature of the arrangement, were trying to carve a private space, a home, out of the tiny pods. They weren't always concerned with the demands of the public entity, the business that shared the loft with them. Linnell and Ochel, on the other hand, at first willingly sacrificed their private lives for the good of their new company. But that willingness waned, worn down in part by being middlemen between the two halves of their home/workplace.

Bringing work, clients, meetings, and the connections of technology into our homes imports the public realm into our private fiefdoms.

In setting up this lifestyle, Ochel and Linnell unwittingly gave up the privacy that's long been associated with home. They built a glass house, where they lived under the unblinking eye of their student-roommates, clients, employees, and even each other. In talking to them, I began to wonder whether many other Americans effectively are doing the same thing. Bringing work, clients, meetings, and the connections of technology into our homes imports the public realm into our private fiefdoms. This new life chips away at the private nature of home. It threatens to turn our sanctuaries into glass houses.

Our desire for privacy ebbs and flows according to different seasons of life, but the need is always there. Children learn quickly that going to the bathroom is a private act, and begin to zealously guard their privacy, tittering at any mention of bodily functions. At life's end, one of the most painful aspects of being unable to care for yourself is losing your privacy. When my mother-in-law was dying of cancer, one of my most uncomfortable memories was seeing her emaciated body in her last days at home. I hadn't known her for many years, and I wanted to help nurse her. Even though she was amazingly strong and serene amid her pain, it seemed like a terrible intrusion to look at her as I helped move her on her side or back. I became an accomplice to the indignity of her illness. To be without privacy is to be without a kind of second skin.

Privacy is also closely connected with secrecy, the hiding of dirty or bad actions from public guard. "Behind closed doors" has a threatening connotation. Still, while privacy can be used in negative ways, it's too crucial to wholly give up. "An important reason that we have envelopes around first-class letters or doors on rooms is not to protect the guilty," writes Gary Marx, a professor emeritus at MIT and expert on privacy issues. "It is because control over personal information is important to our concept of human dignity."

Nor does privacy necessarily breed aloneness. Private moments can be shared by family members, friends, even strangers. At the small library where I often read or write, the main study room is used by up to a dozen others. Still, these hours are more private than many others in my life. My thoughts are rarely interrupted. When I've had a morning in this library, I feel sated. Privacy protects us, without cutting us off from others. It enables us to go back out in the public world recharged. "At its best, privacy shields and nurtures what is unique and authentic in people, while its absence or its violation often contributes to dehumanizing them," Janna Malamud Smith writes in her book *Private Matters: In Defense of the Personal Life*. "Privacy shelters, and thus offers sustenance to fragile virtues."

It's telling that writers often compare privacy to a dwelling. For many cultures today, the place most linked with privacy is the home. But from the sixteenth century even into the early twentieth century, Western houses were more public places. During these centuries, many well-to-do households included servants, apprentices, employees, extended family members, and long-visiting friends of the family that lived there. In the Middle Ages, both poor and rich largely led a public life. Children were conceived, born, and raised all in front of others, often in one room. "Life was a public affair, and just as one did not have a strongly developed self-consciousness, one did not have a room of one's own," writes Witold Rybczynski.

Only as paid work gradually migrated outside the home did family life become more intimate and homes grow private, marked by a division of space into public and private halves. By the Industrial Age, the home was idealized as a sanctuary from the world. "Home became a refuge from that public world of work, where the nurturing, expressive ambiance created by mother and wife served as a retreat for all (except women, perhaps)," writes Christena Nippert-Eng. Suburbia, with its developments of carefully separated houses removed from the city, took the idea of the private home to its apotheosis.

Increasingly, the assumption today in both public and private arenas is that you have to make the private space yourself.

Today, it's almost impossible to pick up a newspaper without seeing an article about a new threat to Americans' privacy. One furor arose because an Internet advertising company tracked individual consumers' web activity in order to send them highly targeted ads. Some health-related web sites share consumer information with third parties, although they promise not to do so. Chefs now use computers and cameras to monitor diners' spending and eating habits. Such tracking of personal data intrudes on people's privacy by stripping away their anonymity, unasked.

Less attention is paid to the privacy of time and space. I particularly detest the ubiquitous video monitors set up in airport waiting areas, on airplanes, in restaurants, and even in doctor's offices. (And now video screens with ads and news are being added to elevators. The idea is that, since people don't talk on elevators, they'll welcome something to watch.) To advertisers, these moments of transition seem like empty spaces. But these jabbering screens often interrupt me when I'm talking with a family member or thinking about the journey or work ahead of me, moments that, even if silent, aren't dead or useless. Moreover, I'm given no chance to decide whether I want these screens to surround me. I'm expected to turn away if I don't want to see or hear their dancing lights and noises. (That's a feat, given their plenitude.)

At home, I theoretically have a say in whether telemarketers call during dinner or companies litter my doorstep with junk mail. I can take the time-consuming step of asking them not to contact me. In effect, I must erect walls and gates if I want to control my private space. In a seminal *Harvard Law Review* article in 1890, Louis Brandeis and Samuel Warren defined privacy as the "right to be left alone." Increasingly, the assumption today in both public and private arenas is that you have to make the private space yourself. It's sort of like saying that trespassing is fine, until the homeowner puts up a fence.

This changing view of private space illuminates why people aren't even aware of how they're eroding the privacy of their own homes. If they don't actively create the walls, as Colin Ochel ultimately did in refusing to give out his home number or answer work e-mails on weekends, then it's assumed that they are accessible. Even if people seek to be available to others, their accessibility snowballs, until they're giving up far more privacy than they'd intended. They think they're leaving the door ajar, but it's blown wide open, as Jan Monti discovered when she set up a consulting and outplacement business in her Seattle home.

Monti had always worked in a corporate setting, so friends immediately warned her that if she went out on her own, she'd be lonely. But she didn't end up feeling isolated. She felt invaded. "My home is my sanctuary," says Monti, a soft-spoken and easygoing woman. "It's where I go to decompress and not worry about how I act and how I look." But with strangers coming into her home, she found that she had to work hard to be more formal and professional. She felt compromised and awkward in the place where she had been used to feeling most relaxed.

Our cultural norms are still largely predicated on the segmentist model of separate realms for home and work. That's one reason why balancing home and work creates such stress for most people. Perhaps as the lines between these realms crumble, we'll eventually grow more accustomed to changing our behavior according to the needs of the moment—not the dictates of the place. We won't find it hard, as Jan Monti did, to put on our professional mask for clients at home, then slip it off at day's end to talk to an intimate.

Yet Jan Monti argues for preserving the sanctity of the home, where we can be a different person than we are while working, and I agree. In at least part of our home, we need places and times that allow us to recoup, restore our dignity, or escape from the gaze of others, especially in an age when the outside world is fast-paced, demanding, and stimulating. In describing her experiences to me one winter's day, Monti begins by talking of "forced intimacy." At first, I'm alarmed, assuming she's referring to a rude client who sat too close to her on the couch or worse. But gradually, I begin to understand. No matter how well-dressed she was, or how well-scoured her home, she couldn't prevent her clients from seeing her private domain—her bathroom, her kitchen, her Persian cat. They couldn't help but drink in these details of her life and make judgments. "You know you're giving them a lot of extra data to evaluate you as a professional that's totally unrelated to the service they're getting," says Monti. "They're looking at your bathroom, and they're thinking, 'What a crummy choice of wallpaper.' As a human it's hard not to make judgments about people based on their personal surroundings."

To a degree, Jan Monti could control her clients' exposure to her private life by dressing in a suit and closing a door or two in her house. But her clients always saw more than she wanted them to see. She felt unfairly exposed. After eighteen months, she moved her growing business to a rented office in downtown Seattle. Now, she keeps business to a minimum at home, even leaving the room if her husband takes a business call at home.

Today, they can follow you all over the world.

Natalie Bee, secretary

Jan Monti was able to turn her home back into a sanctuary because she recognized what was wrong—and because she was her own boss. But what about the many people who don't call the shots in their work lives? As I pondered the issue of privacy at home, I began thinking about secretaries, the women (for they're still mostly women) who have more decision-making power and status than ever before, yet still must answer to one or more bosses. Many are increasingly connected to their employers via e-mail, voice mail, pagers, and cell phones. I asked how this newfound connectivity was affecting their private lives.

Natalie Bee didn't read work e-mails at home six months ago. But Bee, an executive secretary at a South Carolina medical center, now often spends up to an hour a day at home reading job-related e-mail. "Ten years ago, I couldn't ever have seen myself sitting up at midnight and checking my e-mails," she says in a lilting drawl. "Before you go to the mailbox and you get your mail, you go to the computer and get it!" Bee also spends thirty to forty-five minutes at home several times a week checking office voice mails, even while on vacation or when she's sick. She carries a cell phone for both work and pleasure, and wears a beeper several times a month, sometimes during her lunch hour. She's always been a hard worker, and she's chosen to use most of this technology because she feels that her position as a senior secretary demands it. And, since she leaves work early sometimes in order to go to night school, she believes she owes her employer extra time.

But she knows that this constant connectivity to work has changed her life. "Before, when you went home, you enjoyed family time and whatever else," she muses wistfully. Now, her home is no longer a refuge. "I don't even know what it is to relax anymore," she says.

Secretaries from Michigan to Kentucky told similar stories. They often worked as hard at home as they did at the office and spoke of being "followed" by work—a way of life that is becoming increasingly common across occupations. A national study by the Families and Work Institute found that more than forty percent of employees use technology—cell phones, pagers, e-mail, etc.—often or very often for work purposes during their time off. Only thirty percent of employees said they never have to be accessible to their jobs when not at work.

Some secretaries are thrilled by their highly connected status. Brenda Hendron, a single mother who works for a high-tech company in suburban Boston, checks e-mail and voice mail from home daily. As she dresses her daughter for school in the morning, she often gets 7 a.m. phone calls from bosses asking for their day's schedule. She explains, "We all have cell phones. Everybody's reachable." Describing herself as "aggressive, energetic, and fast-paced," Hendron says she loves feeling part of the "executive team." Her mother worries that she works too hard. But at the moment, working at home provides Hendron with an exciting alternative to hanging out or watching TV. She says that since she's divorced, she doesn't have the burden of wondering whether she should be talking to her husband, instead of working at night.

Being available around the clock is becoming an unwritten rule for success.

The tools of technology are seductive. I recall taking a flight from Washington, D.C., to New York on a cold Friday evening one December. The plane was delayed on the tarmac for a couple of hours, so when the pilot gave the go-ahead for passengers to use their electronic devices, a sea of commuters in Burberry trenchcoats started yammering on cell phones. Phone-less, I sheepishly pulled out my Christmas cards. Cell phones and the like say to others, "You are needed. You're important." Even more, such tools symbolize a willingness to keep up with accelerating workloads. They are badges of honor in today's work world, because being available around the clock is becoming an unwritten rule for success. That's why secretaries who are living up to these expectations feel proud that they are doing a good job, even as they grow uneasy about the cost to their home lives.

Even those who want to set limits on their accessibility find it difficult, if not impossible, to do so in an era when there are few rules to protect private life. Usually, people assume that they can control their accessibility by turning technology off and on. But that's not as easy as it sounds, and it takes constant work. It's a bit like saying, "I won't get in a car accident, because I'm a good driver." What about all the other drivers on the road? Turning off a cell phone or a computer is a temporary fix. People who own technology must scramble to build new barriers, and constantly adjust the degree of access others have to them—or lose their privacy.

The secretaries I talked to reminded me of the old woman in a children's book, *Cats and Robbers*. The old woman can't sleep because her house is overrun with squeaking mice, so she opens the windows to let in a multitude of cats. She can't stand the howling cats, so she lets in . . . and so on. To keep up with their accelerating workloads, the secretaries adopt one technology after another. As a result, they give up more and more of their private space, uneasily or unwittingly. One secretary proudly told me that she's been checking her e-mails daily at home for three years. When I ask her what she did at home before she got the computer, her mask of cheer slips. "Probably got some rest," she says wearily. "You get tired of it at some points." Still, she scorns people who "don't have a home life," who work all day, eat dinner, and start working again in the evening. I gently ask, what's the difference between those people and you? "I'm just checking in, they're doing reports," she says, surprised at my question.

Ironically, many of the secretaries singled out "reports" or any quiet, creative work as enjoyable—not a burden—to bring home. Janet Bell, who works for Hewlett-Packard in San Jose, said she happily brings this kind of work to her remote cottage in the woods—the place she calls her "protected zone." Such work can be done in quiet moments, within the rhythm of home lives. It's work that reflects the best parts of the secretaries' jobs: areas of responsibility and individual input. Since these projects tend to be more private and easily controlled, they are less apt to puncture the sanctuary of the home.

In contrast, the work of accessibility—e-mails, voice mails, phone calls, beepers—tends to bring the outside, public world hurtling into the home. The more mobile a worker is, the more he or she turns into a worker on-call, concluded one team of researchers from Santa Clara University. "In today's workplace, we've snuck up on employees and placed them on-call. . . . It has a glorious, heroic sound to it," observes Beth Sawi, chief administrative officer at Charles Schwab & Co., Inc. "Today you're kind of free, you're kind of not." That's why many of the secretaries I spoke with felt that work "followed" them. "He's going to search me out wherever I am," secretary Cynthia Lively says of her boss, who e-mails Lively as well as calling her on her cell and home phones. "It's much harder to relax. There's all this instant communications." Lively sometimes finds it hard to sleep after working in the evening, and misses her old habit of curling up with a fun book. "It seems like I'm always on the computer, checking e-mail, or bringing work home," she says.

This way of life changes the perimeters of a worker's private time. "The borders between action and inaction, on- and off-duty and public and private that were available with the 'natural' rhythms of day and night, weekends and holidays, are less evident for more people who are 'on-call' regardless of the time or where they are," writes Gary Marx. As I've noted, farmers and craftsmen mostly looked to natural cues—from the daily path of the sun to cycles of the moon and the seasons—in mapping out patterns of rest and work in their lives. As work moved away from home, machines and electric light severed labor from these cues, leading to the adoption of weekends and vacations as times of rest. Now that weekends and vacations are less defined yet the sun and seasons hold little sway over our lives, just when in the twenty-first century will we rest?

I worried when I first began to see companies offer home computers for little or no cost to their employees. If it's difficult for a secretary to keep from being on-call twenty-four hours a day, it will be no easier for an auto worker or a flight attendant to protect their homes from intrusions. Ford and Delta, the pioneers in this endeavor, stress that their programs are voluntary, although the dirt-cheap cost and encouragement from the company to enroll ensure that the computers are distributed company-wide. Once connected, then what?

The companies say they won't monitor their employees' home Internet use, yet I wonder about management's expectations. "We're looking at this as an extension of our business tools, so people will be able to be more closely aligned with the company," says Delta spokesman Kip Smith. It's true that all workers, up and down the corporate ladder, need to be tech-savvy these days. Yet "closely aligning" workers with the company could quickly place employees on-call. As part of some company computer giveaway programs, for example, workers will begin taking training programs home to do at night. What happens when Joe Autoworker doesn't see the shift change posted at 10 p.m. on his home computer? What if an off-duty flight attendant uses the company computer in her home to send a racist e-mail to a coworker? One thing is clear: such giveaway programs extend "the long arm of the workplace," says sociologist Arlie Hochschild.

Armed with a court order, Northwest Airlines in 1999 hired a consultant to search the home computer hard drives of twenty union flight attendants after the airline experienced sick-outs during a long-running contract dispute. (Most of the computers were handed over at locations other than the attendants' homes.) Northwest said it had no interest in the personal files of its workers but was entitled to see if there was evidence of a sick-out conspiracy. After the contract was settled, the airline ordered its copies of the hard drives destroyed.

Still, the case raises important questions about privacy and the home, as do the computer giveaway programs. In a world where technology is fast making workers on-call, we should think carefully about the price we pay for making all places, including home, connected.

> We have the ability to rebuild some of the private spaces we have lost. But do we have the will?
>
> Jeffrey Rosen, *The Unwanted Gaze*

Today, the privacy of our homes is easily punctured. Clients see our dirty laundry, literally and figuratively.

Bosses and colleagues interrupt breakfast and bedtime. Work creeps into our thoughts, unseen but needing attention, like e-mail beaming into our computers. Children easily connect to online communities, while barely spending time with family members. How are we coping? Increasingly, a marketplace is being born, where not only personal data but private space and time are being bought and sold, bargained and bartered.

Linda Waali is a troubleshooter, on contract to Microsoft's licensing and anti-piracy department. She helps fix computer problems for customers worldwide, wearing a pager at all times and keeping a cell phone on when she's out of reach of her office or home phones. In exchange for taking this job, she got a substantial raise. "I didn't have to accept this position," she tells me, even as she admits that she can't envision working this way for a long time.

She's rarely called during the night, yet finds that she sleeps fitfully. "I hear the slightest noise, and I wake up. . . . Was that the phone? Was that the pager?" she explains. When we first spoke, she was eagerly awaiting her first vacation without the technology, a weeklong trip to Las Vegas. She yearned for a full night of sleep, a day off without interruption. Bringing the technology along would defeat the purpose of a vacation, she assures me. "In the middle of a hot blackjack run, you want to tell me that China's having connectivity problems?" Yet even arranging the vacation wasn't easy. She had to find a substitute on-call worker, then badger her bosses for weeks before they gave the final okay to the trip. Once sold, Linda Waali found her privacy hard to buy back, even for one week.

Humans have long bought privacy, especially at home. Fences, walls, burglar alarms, and locks have been intended to keep out robbers and voyeurs. Answering machines, caller ID, and other tools are used to manage accessibility. Politicians and celebrities must go a step further, trading privacy in pursuit of fame, power, and wealth. But never before have people like you and me faced greater pressure and opportunity to sell our own privacy. "We will increasingly face tradeoffs between maintaining our privacy and getting better service by giving some of it up," writes William J. Mitchell, dean of MIT's School of

Architecture and Planning, in his book *e-topia*. (Taking this trend a step further, a string of Internet companies are offering people the chance to earn commissions by including ads in their e-mails. That means people now have the chance to sell their friend's privacy, not just their own.) Most frightening is the rise in people willing to sell, trade, or barter the privacy of their own homes.

Natalie Bee, the South Carolina hospital secretary, remains connected to work night and day because her boss expects her to, and because she wants to live up to these expectations. But she also brings work into her private life as a quid pro quo. Several days a week, she leaves the office early to attend night school. In return, she gives up private time—probably far more than the hours she misses at work. Implicitly, Bee is striking a bargain with her workplace. In order to acquire the flexibility to pursue a life outside work, she and many others of us are bartering away a growing segment of their private lives.

If privacy is only for people with something to hide, then its value has surely fallen.

The marketplace for privacy helps explain another modern phenomenon: webcams. I first started talking with Linda Waali because she had purchased one of these tiny cameras, becoming one of the five million Americans to do so by 2000. A webcam broadcasts a live video picture to the web, for all the connected world to see. Certainly, some of the cameras are being set up for suspect reasons. But it intrigued me that people who consider themselves private, who are worlds away from being porn queens or exhibitionists, also have installed them. I thought their reasoning would tell me something about the changing nature of privacy, especially at home.

When Waali is at the office, she trains her camera on her five cats' favorite sunny corner. "It's a way of catching up on my kids," she jokes. She also keeps the camera running while she's at home, a habit that she calls sharing "a slice of life" with the outside world. She doesn't appear all that often, or for very long before the camera, which is set up in her home office. She'll wave to her mother, or come into view when crossing the room. Yet its presence changes her home life. Waali keeps a hat hanging on the doorknob of her home office, which she flings over the camera if she wants privacy. She's considering posting a sign on the door in order to warn guests when the camera's running. In setting up the camera, she must constantly navigate between the off-camera, private world and the "slice of life" she puts on public display.

Still, she's adamant that she hasn't compromised her privacy, saying she chooses the camera's view, can turn it off at any time, and has nothing to hide. "I'm not going to take a shower in front of the camera," she told me. "But if you want to see what I'm going to have for dinner, go ahead. Does mac-and-cheese thrill you?"

Other webcam users I interviewed felt just as casual about the public viewing of their home lives. People often told me that originally they signed up so an elderly relative could see video of their children. But strangers on the web can watch them, and the software even enables camera owners to see how many "hits" their site is getting. Truetech, a Dutch company that makes webcam software, ironically gets a constant string of e-mails from users who are outraged that they are being watched! Still, the webcam users I spoke with were amused, intrigued, or uncaring that unseen eyes were watching their homes. "It's just life," computer programmer Lou Lange told me. "It's just me going through my paces." This view told me a lot about how privacy had changed in this country, and why people would allow their jobs to increasingly intrude on their home life. It's easier to sell, barter, or fritter away something that's no longer held sacred. If privacy is only for people with something to hide, then its value has surely fallen.

Fallen, but not disappeared. Few people are willing to squander all of the private spaces in their lives. Most webcam users don't run their cameras twenty-four hours a day, nor do they set them up in every corner of their houses. Most secretaries admitted, after we'd talked for a while, that they were chafing at their electronic leashes. I didn't mention the words "sanctuary" or "refuge" in interviews, but these words surfaced deep into conversations. With varying degrees of success, people are trying to retain some control over the intrusion of the public into the sanctuary of their homes.

Colin Ochel, the computer animator, held off for a year before allowing a laptop in his new apartment. Although he now uses it just to surf the Net for pleasure and order takeout food, the presence of the machine has changed his home. "It's weird now. It's becoming . . ." he pauses, fumbling for words. "Technology is in my home, whereas before, it was a complete sanctuary." Still, he tentatively concludes that he's better at drawing boundaries after life in the pods. He believes he's ready to reopen the doors of home to work.

Just before I first met Ochel, he bought a weekend home, a 160-year-old house in Newport, Rhode Island. The second time we talk, he slumps wearily in his chair, clad in a torn white sweater. But he grows visibly excited as he outlines his plans to make this summer home a virtual office. At the top of the house, he'll turn a sunlit room into both a painting studio and his home office. Eventually, he'd like to live there during the summers, maybe visiting New York weekly. "I can shut work off when I want to," he says. "I'm not afraid of mixing it all together." His only fear is loneliness. "I've always been scared of that, I've always been scared of the isolation," Ochel admits. He got burned in his live/work space and senses encroaching intrusions in his first home, his sanctuary. So he's taking great care to make sure that in Newport he'll have access to the world, but it will have the least access possible to him.

Many people are turning to this method of survival in order to protect a modicum of sanctuary. In the marketplace of privacy, one-way access is attainable to a degree—for those with power. A secretary may not stand a chance of limiting her boss's access to her, but the boss has the power to carve out private time. This dance of accessibility even occurs within families, Jan English-Lueck has found. An anthropologist at San Jose State University, she has been studying highly connected Silicon Valley families for a decade. The prevalence of the strategy of one-way access "increasingly leads to the use of home as an environment in which interruptions can be carefully managed, even between family members," she observes.

Turning technology on and off in order to preserve the refuge of home, however, can lead to an increased willingness to turn people on and off. With call waiting, for example, recipients of telephone calls are effectively opening and closing doors to others, depending on whether they wish to speak with them. The recipient of the phone call controls the access. I'm also struck by the attitude people often have toward others in chat rooms: they are disposable. One webcam owner told me he's quite adept at judging whether he wants to continue a friendship on the web. How long does that take? "Twenty-five minutes," he said.

Perhaps a kind of privacy can be forged in this way, but if carried too far, this becomes a fragile privacy born out of power and control, not mutual respect. Stephen L. Talbott, editor of the influential online newsletter *NetFuture*, argues forcefully for the preservation of privacy based on the "lowering of our eyes." Talbott believes that privacy based on high walls and fences, or symbolically, caller ID or answering machines, is a kind of false privacy. He's mostly talking about data protection, but his thoughts resonate for people trying to find private times and spaces in their lives. "Privacy, after all, is scarcely relevant to the individual living behind a chainlink fence," he writes. "It can be a concern and a value only where we present ourselves to each other. The 'space' we ask for when we ask for privacy, is a space fashioned within and defended by a respectful community. There is no other enduring defense."

Privacy protects us, allowing us to nurture our most intimate relations with others and with ourselves. . . .

As part of a winter spent studying our city, my second grader had to interview her family members. She asked questions about various landmarks and the apartment building in which we lived. Then she asked us, "What is your favorite place in New York?" I mulled it over, torn between naming my favorite museum or the outdoor ice skating rink where we spend many Saturday mornings. My seven-year-old and four-year-old, on the other hand, didn't hesitate. "Home," they answered. There wasn't even a close second in their opinions.

I was surprised that I hadn't even thought of that answer. My sentiments leaned more toward the outside world, where I could immerse myself in an activity totally unrelated to work. *Metropolis* magazine found a similar attitude when its editors questioned 360 people about where they go to find privacy. The respondents said they find privacy by gardening, taking a walk or a bath, going to sleep, or waiting until late at night when they're alone in the house.

"Privacy is not necessarily something people associate with place," wrote editor Akiko Busch, noting how attitudes toward privacy had evolved markedly from just a generation ago. "Rather, it may be defined by a change in activity or by a specific time." When I read this, I thought of a secretary who giggled as she told me how she finds private time. "It sounds kind of sick—but I love to shovel snow," said Sue Nowicki. "It takes your mind away. I can be in Hawaii, even as I shovel snow."

Nowicki, who works at a small college in northern Michigan, turned in her pager a few months before our interview and began limiting her time spent working at home. She wanted to return to the hobbies she used to enjoy, sculpting and sewing quilts. "I had a reality check," she said. "I wasn't having fun at home anymore." In her basement, near her home office, she has a crafts room where she deliberately does not work. "It's my own little refuge," she says.

The home is no longer idealized as a castle, no longer an impermeable oasis shielding us from work and our fellow man. And that is good. The Industrial Age ideal of home as a private fiefdom, while not fully realized, inspired stifling social conventions and a schism between two crucial realms—work and home. Yet domestic privacy is too important to be entirely left behind as a new century unfolds. Privacy protects us, allowing us to nurture our most intimate relations with others and with ourselves, and we instinctively know this. That is why so many of us are uneasy when we bring work and clients home, and stay accessible to others night and day. We are not content to live in glass houses. We are trying to preserve a measure of privacy in our increasingly permeable homes.

Creating a marketplace for privacy, however, is a dangerous solution. When we negotiate not just personal data but time and space in the domestic realm, we are turning the privacy of our homes into a commodity. Those with power can control access to themselves. Others will barter and trade in this market as best they can. Ultimately, we all lose by erecting virtual versions of fences and walls— call waiting, caller ID, voice mail—or by selling our privacy to our employers. Instead, we need to revalue domestic privacy, rekindle our mutual respect for the refuge of home. A boss who sends an e-mail on Saturday sends an implicit message devaluing home. A routine call to a coworker who is on vacation undermines his privacy.

To revalue domestic privacy, we would do well to look anew at time. Just as today's architecture of home-work teaches us about the importance of keeping a place for home, so our increasing techno-accessibility should open our eyes to the importance of preserving time for home. Being "on-call" via cell phone, e-mail, pager, and fax breaks down the temporal boundaries that mark periods of rest, intimacy, peace—private moments and hours that allow us to create a home that truly is a refuge. Again, the time and place for home can be flexible and changing. In this day and age, few of us will ever want or be able to create a home that is purely domestic, private, and separate from the world. I have sacrificed corners of my living room and bedroom to work, but as a result, I'm trying to keep my dining room consciously "home"—an intersection of private time and space.

Making time for home is not easy, but it's possible. Echoing Danelle Guthrie, Jan Monti chose to redraw the boundaries between work and home by moving her business to a separate office. Sue Nowicki turned in her pager and began limiting her time spent working at home. Colin Ochel is still experimenting. He's introduced technology into his apartment, but keeping the flow of work there to a trickle. He's determined to create a second refuge in a far-off home, connected to work but separate. After living a wholly public life, he has a growing respect for the privacy needed to create home. And perhaps if others respect this privacy, he will not have to make his home into a fortress.

Diary: Cell-Phoning on the Hayride

I rarely like to do two things at once. I've always tried to do my work and then play. Even juggling two stories at one time irritates me. I just can't envision myself making cell phone calls on the nursery school pumpkin patch trip. Or is it just a matter of getting used to it?

One mother on the school trip quietly made cell phone calls even on the hayride. Was that better than not being there? How many calls are too many? Long ago when I worked as an editor in the evenings, one of my bosses used to call me as he gave his toddler a bath. (I used to wonder whether he'd electrocute her if he dropped the phone.) At the time, this seemed very unusual. Few people blended work and home to that extent. It looked like he was an overachiever who couldn't turn work off once he got home. In contrast, the mother on the pumpkin patch trip drew no irritated glares or stares. In fact, I recall that a father was making cell phone calls on the hayride as well. We are growing more accustomed to the sight of people dividing themselves between places—taking care of business while physically remaining right next to you.

But the ability to have a "dual presence" raises the question of when we need to be really here, or there. When a commuter is on the nightly train, using a cell phone to finish up a bit of work on the way home, he's mentally "there" and physically "here" on the train. The trouble is, his thoughts and voice are most distinctly "here" for all other commuters to hear!

My local paper carries a weekly column of anecdotes about New York City life sent in by residents and tourists. Lately, I've often noticed stories concerning cell phones on buses. (They don't yet work on the subway.) One day, a reader told how a caller loudly phoned home to ask if her family wanted salmon or chicken for supper that night. Not long into the conversation, an irritated bus rider shouted "Salmon!", prompting other passengers to take up the cry, "Salmon! Salmon! Salmon!" Unconsciously or not, the riders were yanking this woman back into the physical context of her call—the bus—and reminding her that her actions affected them too.

The mom on the hayride talked so discreetly that her calls may have escaped the notice of most other parents. Yet she was entangling herself in two social situations as well. During her calls, part of her remained with her daughter, part of her stayed accessible to work. If she hadn't taken the cell phone, she would have had to miss the field trip, or miss work to go on the outing. But is partly being there good enough, for either her child or her work? That's a tough question. I have a cell phone, and I once took it along while shepherding my daughter to a friend's birthday party. To my horror, the business call I was waiting for came through while I was in the bathroom. I literally had to pull up my pants, run out of the room with the ringing phone, and feign normalcy as I answered. While glad that I caught the call, I can't say that I was "all there" during the party, before, during, or even after my conversation.

I've never made a phone call on a bus, but I used to call friends while walking to and from the bus stop, feeling gleeful that I could slip in a social call during this "dead time." I don't do that anymore. During the call, too many unpredictables occurred, leading me to cut short the calls. Or I'd get to my front door and hurriedly end the chat so I could see my children. I began to think, why call friends at times when I expect *them* to adhere to my circumstances?

The cell phone makes so many of our activities portable, which is good. But being divided between two places puts us in two contexts. We don't like to think of it that way. We assume that we may freely choose between the two situations, tuning out one while attending to the other and vice versa. Yet we are involved in both situations, and we run the risk of being fair to no one, not even ourselves. During my calls on my walks home, I seemed to be usually the one who got to choose whether my "here" or their "there" mattered more. I wanted others to be accessible to me, although I wasn't always comfortable being accessible to others.

Nowadays as I walk home from the bus stop, I turn off my cell phone and let my mind wander. As I amble along beside Central Park, I try to notice the pastel colors of the sky at sunset, or the phase of the rising moon, or the hurried gait of my fellow commuters. I find that the "here" and "there" of my body and my mental wanderings no longer clash.

THREE

Orphaning Domesticity:

Of Apron Strings
and Hotel Living

It is not in goods that the contemporary household is poor, but in comfort and care.

Cheryl Mendelson, *Home Comforts*

I still remember the apron. It was white, ruffled, and given to me, the bride-to-be, at a shower held by a bevy of my mother-in-law's friends. I opened the box and saw it, folded neatly and tucked into tissue paper. If given by a friend, I would have treated the apron as a joke, a good laugh at what I was not. But this gift, offered earnestly by a friendly band of fifty-somethings, was no joke. They were trying to equip me for the set of roles—wife, homemaker, mother—that had been their primary identity. They were inducting me into a club they naturally assumed I was joining. I was aghast at being passed a torch that I had no wish to carry.

The apron is long gone. I threw it away as soon as I could, and probably have suffered many a stain or spot at the stove over the years as a result of my youthful defiance. Yet more than a decade later, I'd do it again, and I think many people in their twenties, thirties, forties, and even fifties would do the same. For both men and women, the apron symbolizes a domesticity of the past, a view of household work that at once fascinates, discomforts, and even repels us. The apron symbolizes a time when the home

61

was a feminine world, a time when women were tied to domestic matters by their very apron strings.

Nowadays, most women don't want to wear that apron; men don't want to put it on either. Women have worked outside the home for as long as factories have been humming, and still held on to homemaking as a primary identity. No longer. A majority of women share the role of breadwinner with men, and derive as much or more fulfillment from their work as their homemaking. Men are edging back into the household involvement they prized in colonial times, yet most would wince if called domestic. Today, both men and women are orphaning domesticity. Housecleaning is denigrated and cooking is an elite, weekend hobby at best. Domestic gurus like Martha Stewart preach veneration of the domestic arts, but in a form that's so exclusive, time-consuming, and expensive that the outcome is a caricature of homemaking. Increasingly, the middle classes pay strangers to mow their lawns, clean their toilets, cook their meals, tidy their closets, count their sit-ups, run their errands. They pay others to weave the fabric of their home lives.

How can we forge a modern idea of domesticity that frees women and still venerates the intimacy of home?

I'll never wear an apron, and I'm not the only parent who rocks the crying baby at midnight, bakes the birthday cakes, or cooks Christmas dinner. Still, I pay someone to clean my house, and I wouldn't mind sending out for take-out more often. I don't consider myself "domestic," a term that has a pejorative ring. So, I wonder what domesticity means today? Are chores meaningless drudgework or the threads that bind the tapestry of our home lives? Does outsourcing your domestic life really produce elusive quality time, or does it turn family members of all types— gay couples, single parents, stepfamilies—into roommates no more connected than occupants of a group house? Most important, I want to know how we can forge a modern idea of domesticity that frees women and still venerates the intimacy of home. These questions drive to the heart of what it means to have a home.

Like most people, my view of homemaking is deeply caught up in my parents' attitudes toward keeping house. Saturday yard work, cigarette burns on the sofa, six o'clock suppers—these rituals and images colored my early world. In childhood, I first learned what it takes to make a home—or not.

I don't recall ever seeing my mother vacuum. She had asthma, so perhaps that's why. But I think her allergies to housework ran deeper than that. She was the oldest daughter in a family of nine, and by her twenties I think she'd done enough housework, cooking, and domestic chores for a lifetime. She also taught school after my twin sister and I began kindergarten. At seven years old, we started packing our own lunches and unloading the dishwasher. Soon after, we did all the vacuuming, dusting, laundry, and scouring of ashtrays—my personal least-favorite. In elementary school, we were allowed the luxury of buying the thirty-cent cafeteria lunch once a week. One day, I remember realizing with surprise that it was better than my mother's cooking.

It wasn't that she couldn't do all these things. We'd see glimpses of her prowess at times. If I was making a cake, invariably I'd fail in the frosting department and she'd put down her newspaper, come to the kitchen, and in minutes turn my lumpy sugar mess into a perfect frosting. She knew which stains to treat with hot water and which with cold, and she knew the Latin names of the plants in the straggly home garden she never touched.

We had pretty high housekeeping standards, unlike other neighbors whose houses were carpeted with furballs and whose windows were smeared. It was my neatnik Dad, also a teacher, who showed my sister and me how to clean the last bits of food out of the kitchen sink and wipe the crumbs out from under the toaster. He could never get my mother to sort through the mail piled up in the kitchen or throw away old newspapers, but he'd insist that we go back and catch the spots we'd missed while vacuuming or dusting.

Still, I chafed at his lessons, and never really appreciated housekeeping. I was neat, but barely cleaned my myriad domiciles as a single adult, and supper in those days usually meant yogurt and salads, perhaps a plain bowl of hot rice. It was college living, stretched out years after graduation. After John and I lived together, then married, we shared the chores, although I was the second-string domestician. He's always been the more assured cook, and knows how to keep a washing machine in submission. He notices when the toilets need cleaning sooner than I do. Am I lazy? Or do I secretly feel that to slip too eagerly into this role is to accept that apron I threw out long ago?

I see evidence all around me that many other women feel similarly of two minds when it comes to keeping house. When it was my turn to host my monthly book club, I made banana muffins. But I thought long and hard before doing so. I like baking, and that morning I didn't have time to visit a bakery before the other mothers were to arrive. But I knew that making muffins was also making a statement; I just didn't know how much of one. From the moment somebody found out that the muffins were homemade, the talk about them hardly stopped. "You have to try these! She made them!" the women called to arriving guests before they'd even taken off their coats. No one sneered. They praised the muffins to the hilt and two people copied down the recipe by hand. But their surprise and my discomfort show how conflicted women are about domesticity.

Domestic work has become a hidden, somewhat embarrassing hobby. It's sort of like confessing that you'd secretly love to be Amish. Katy-Duke Chamberlin, a chef in Washington, D.C., once wore capri pants that were admired by friends one evening. But after she admitted that she'd sewn on the fashionable swatch of fabric at the hem, her friends were baffled. "It was beyond them," says Chamberlin, who spent the rest of the evening answering questions about whether she'd made her purse, her shirt, etc. One day, I saw an article by a young woman who loved cooking, but felt that her domesticity scared off commitment-phobic men. Giving her boyfriend a birthday cake in front of his cool coworkers at MTV was one of the hardest things she'd ever done, she wrote. "Someday I'll feel comfortable coming out of the closet," she wrote.

Our homes are the center of our lives.

Cheryl Mendelson

It's spring, and I'm sitting in a dimly lit Hungarian pastry shop in northern Manhattan waiting for someone who knows all about angst and domesticity. Cheryl Mendelson sweeps in, late for our meeting, and almost immediately, before I have a chance to ask any questions, she breathlessly offers a defense of her book *Home Comforts: The Art and Science of Keeping House*. The book, billed as the first housekeeping manual written in a century, is selling like hotcakes, but has also drawn fire. A book on stain removal and household management incensing the critics? I'm intrigued.

"They think I'm saying, 'Women, back to the kitchens! Put on those aprons!' This was not my idea at all," says Mendelson, who, with her sandy brown hair and soothing voice, at first looks like any other playground mother. When she begins to warm to her subject, however, it's clear she's no Héloise. Mendelson, a lawyer with a Ph.D. in philosophy, is actually approaching housekeeping with intellect.

In her book, she begins with an impassioned lament for the decline of housekeeping, arguing for its importance in our society. She confesses how she kept her love of domestic arts a secret, but rediscovered their importance a few years ago. "Our homes are the center of our lives, and we should allow time and resources to make the most of them that we can, and to care for them in a way that consolidates and elaborates their meaning for each of us," she writes. She links housekeeping with the very foundations of a democratic society. How can citizens govern themselves if they can't take care of themselves and their homes, she asks?

Nowhere does Mendelson address any of her encyclopedic advice solely to women. In fact, she hired a housecleaner while she wrote her book, a decision that she asserts shouldn't put a "black mark on my soul." She's trying to venerate the idea of home without tying women to it, and doesn't feel that her message is being heard. In our society, women have been owned by issues surrounding the home for so long that a defense of housekeeping seems automatically to be a promotion for fifties-style homemaking.

Historically, the idea of a feminine cult of domesticity is relatively new, having been created just a century and a half ago. In Medieval Europe, home meant heaven, with life largely a journey to this spiritual homecoming. Even when Protestantism began turning people's focus to the quality of life on earth, homes—thus domesticity—meant little. Few people actually owned a home, and apprentices, servants, lodgers, and children customarily lived apart from their nuclear families. They were homeless, in the modern sense, yet very much a part of the social order of the busy, noisy households that took them in, according to historian John Gillis. In this era, much time was spent in public places; church and community dominated life. The word "homesick" didn't come into use until the late eighteenth century, and even then, initially meant a longing for one's native region. Before the nineteenth century, ghosts tended to haunt bridges and marketplaces, not houses.

Colonial households, too, reflected a greater society ruled by church and community. Men ran the household yet fully shared in the raising of children, taking responsibility, for example, for children's religious education. Women butchered animals, brewed ale, negotiated for family goods, and managed family businesses when their husbands died, according to historian Stephanie Coontz. A few eighteenth-century women worked as blacksmiths, butchers, attorneys, and doctors. Some English women in America could dispose of their own property and act as guardians to the young. Men weren't considered breadwinners, nor were women dependents, notes Coontz.

By the nineteenth century, the Western idea of home and women's place in the world had vastly changed. As I write, I'm sitting in a library before a British engraving from 1800 entitled "The Fruits of Early Industry and Oeconemy." A poem below explains how a grown son and his father are counting the "well-earned plenty" from their business dealings, although they're clearly at home. Nearby, the son's well-dressed young wife dangles grapes before a small boy, while another toddler frolics with a dog. In this early image of domesticity, women and household matters are peripheral to the male-dominated wage economy. Separated from the tempestuous world, home is a refuge where men can bask in their profits and then go back out to make more. Home is a distinctly feminine realm, where women control the family's moral and emotional life—not to mention the stove, sewing basket, and chamber pots.

Home—it's just a place I come and go. It's not a place I like to spend a lot of time at.

Jim Vanderslice

Karin Collis is picking at the pull-tab of her Diet Coke. A plump, energetic woman with soft, blond hair, it seems hard for her to sit down for long at any time—but especially today. Her nineteen-year-old son has just had his wisdom teeth taken out, and he's upstairs napping on the couch as she talks with me in her basement rec room. She tried to make phone calls at the dentist, but didn't get far. The phone line into her home business is now ringing repeatedly. She's distracted and stressed-out.

But that's just why, over the past few years, she's hired one professional after another to take over her domestic life. She has a cleaning service to scrub her house, a suburban Washington, D.C. mini-mansion where not a knickknack appears out of place. A woman from the "Clutterbuck" agency organizes her closets, while two errand services deliver Christmas gifts or fetch her son's contact lenses. In addition, three part-time personal assistants help run her logo business, and do family errands. Now that she's in the middle of a divorce, Collis is hiring a lawn care service and a chef who will come to her home to cook and freeze dinners for her and her two teenage sons. About the only domestic chore Collis still does is the laundry. When I mention I'll be interviewing a man who delivers Christmas trees door-to-door in her area, Collis sits up, although it's only May. "I'd like to know that number!" she says.

Still, she's torn. She tells me twice in twenty minutes that she came from a very conservative Greek family, where her mother cooked, cleaned, and had dinner on the table promptly at six each night. When Collis began working at a small company some years ago, she tried to keep doing all the housework. But after starting her own business in 1994, she threw in the kitchen towel and began hiring help. To Collis, it seemed that she could run a successful business, or do the housework, not both. Now, she's pleased that she can take her kids to a museum or a friend's house on weekends, rather than doing housework or nagging her sons to do chores. Still, she's chagrined at how her domestic life has turned out.

"I don't think it's an ideal home life for kids," she says, staring at her empty soda can. "I don't like this hectic pace. There's no time for them." Collis misses being able to make a nice meal, but by the time she quits work in the evenings, she's too exhausted to cook more than a few times a week. She doesn't make her sons do chores around the house because she feels guilty that she works such long hours. "You give them a lot of slack, because you don't want another argument," she says. "It's not like a family, where everybody helps out."

Her assistant interrupts to ask about her son's medication, and Collis responds briskly that he must eat before taking any. "There's Jell-O in the fridge—in those little cups," says Collis. She turns back to me. "That's sad," she says, softly. "I can't even make Jell-O."

The specter of the nineteenth-century cult of domesticity haunts women, berating them for their dust bunnies and Chinese takeout. Nevertheless, the truth is that in recent decades, women do far less housework than at any other point in history. In 1965, women kept house thirty hours a week, while in 1995 they did 17.5 hours of housework—including 6.7 hours of cleaning—according to sociologists at the University of Maryland. Men's time spent cleaning rose 240 percent in those 30 years—to 1.7 hours a week. Men are doing more around the house in other ways as well, but women still do what sociologist Arlie Hochschild has called the "second shift"—even if it's a shrinking shift. All in all, nobody's doing much around the house.

And why shouldn't women like Karin Collis want to avoid scouring the toilets and changing the cat box? No matter how loftily portrayed as symbolizing a woman's love for family, housework is often onerous, repetitive, and certainly unappreciated. Women have spent centuries trying to free themselves from the work of running a home, a backbreaking, full-time job before the advent of prepared foods, store-bought clothes, running water, and electricity. One nineteenth-century researcher calculated that a farmer's wife, making eight to ten trips a day to haul water home from a spring, trekked 6,068 miles in forty years. Historian Susan Strasser doesn't romanticize this past life. "Tainted water supplies, rancid food, soot and skin burns from open fires, and full chamber pots offer a more accurate picture of daily life for most people before the twentieth century than the less frequent pleasures of the quilting bee," she writes. Still, she also notes that housework before consumerism involved a great deal of craftsmanship, intimacy, and strong community ties. Women socialized at the well and took pride in their sewing. Households helped each other raise barns or harvest crops. Family members worked side-by-side on chores both pleasant and dull.

Hiring a cleaning service is no black mark on anyone's soul. I pay someone to clean my house and I'm relieved to do so, especially after starting in on these chores at age seven. I also have a part-time nanny. What interests me is the outsourcing of just about every domestic activity, a trend that begins to look like hotel living—at home. I know a woman who has different people come to her house to help her decorate, cut her hair, give her massages, teach her how to use her computer, cater her parties, cook nightly dinners, and care for her children. There's the danger of an emptiness to this kind of living, a temptation to assume that the best qualities of a home—caring, time together—can be bought, not made.

Each time we cook, clean, or mend, we're creating opportunities for being together with those who share our home.

This woman is, you might guess, well-off. But among the middle classes, such upper-crust luxuries as a cook, cleaner, or gardener are no longer rare. Between 1995 and 2000, the number of households using a cleaner—either an individual or a service—rose by 15 percent, to nearly a fifth of households. Demand is growing for personal chefs, who earn $300 to $400 weekly for stocking your freezer with batches of homemade, microwavable meals. The five thousand member U.S. Personal Chef Association got one thousand requests for a chef in 1996, and twenty-two thousand requests in 2000.

Even during a slowing economy, people are willing to hand over almost any domestic work to a stranger. One woman in California does nothing but taxi children around to after-school activities. Sales of prepared Thanksgiving dinners rose forty percent from 1998 to 1999 at Kroger, a supermarket chain. As part of his Washington, D.C.-area Christmas tree delivery service, David Kranich and his employees will haul a chosen specimen inside and even set it in a stand. Yet Kranich gets many requests that he come in and *decorate* the tree as well.

Sitting in Karin Collis' rec room before Collis returns home, her assistant-of-the-day Tobey Martin muses on this new industry. A young woman with long auburn hair and girlish bangs, Martin sometimes helps Collis with personal chores, such as her son's medication, or with administrative work for her logo business. Today, as Martin talks, she is careful to keep up with her afternoon's work: testing a box of old sample pens to see which ones still work. Scribbling away, Martin recalls that when she first set up her own business, Errands Etc., she tried to do everything: walk dogs, shop for clothes, buy groceries. Not only was she run ragged, but she discovered that she was vainly competing with a myriad of new specialists—image consultants, personal shoppers, party planners, dog walkers. Now she sticks to grocery shopping, filing, and running odd errands for her growing client list.

She also finds time for home. She and her husband and infant son eat out several times a week, but other nights her husband cooks. The past weekend, they all planted flowers in their yard, then as her son napped, she and her husband cleaned the house. "If it's time we're spending together as a family, it's enjoyable," she says, reaching for another pen.

The domestic work we often dread—raking the leaves, scouring the kitchen sink, washing the curtains—doesn't necessarily make a house a home. Certainly not. Yet outsourcing domestic life does have a symbolic cost, because such chores in sum are more than just drudgery. In accomplishing seemingly small domestic tasks again and again, we're creating much more than a tidy shelter from the elements. Each time we cook, clean, or mend, we're creating opportunities for talking, for being together with those who share our home. We're creating the glue that binds us to the humans we love. We're recognizing the cyclical nature of life. This doesn't mean that we need to worship Martha Stewart or do all domestic work ourselves. But it's hard to build a home unless people take some time to care for it and for each other. Many women feel guilty that they can't live up to the archaic expectation that they do it all. Yet perhaps their uneasiness also stems from an instinctive understanding of the importance of this work.

During the nineteenth century, as home became the symbolic center of the Victorian universe and women derived their identity from ruling this realm, the role of the American father completely changed. Men became near-strangers at home. Returning home each day to a world now set apart from them, a man became a playmate, visiting judge, disciplinarian, and the biggest child in the family, writes historian John Demos. Today, aren't these the roles that men and women play when they outsource their domestic life? We become intruders in our own homes when we buy designer kitchens that sit untouched, or ask a stranger to decorate our Christmas tree. We try to become our children's friends, not their parents, when we share only play time with them. We become children waiting to be nurtured when we rely on strangers to keep our houses running.

Nor are women alone in recognizing this Faustian bargain. Just as Colin Ochel and Jeff Linnell grew tired of the lack of privacy in their home and work space, men such as Jim Vanderslice are growing uncomfortable with their abandonment of domestic life.

Vanderslice, owner of a Seattle dot-com, doesn't do much more than sleep and occasionally read a book in his 800-square-foot apartment just north of the Space Needle. He eats breakfast and lunch at work, goes out to dinner most nights, and pays others to do his cleaning and laundry. When he wants to feel whole again, he visits married friends and helps them mow their lawns, cook, or fix their boats. At the moment, he's on hold, waiting to make a real home. That would seem like a normal passage of youth, but is questionable for his age, thirty four. "The hard part is figuring out when it stops," he says uneasily.

Vanderslice is hungering for something he once had, a home woven around the intimate work of running the house. The oldest of four children, he knows how to sew and do laundry, and he loved spending hours working in the yard of his family's Connecticut home. He just bought a piece of riverfront land in eastern Washington that he gleefully tells me has a lot of brushwork. For the moment, he's set aside this domestic life, yet finds himself drawn to doing these chores for his friends. He's a stranger in his own home.

Even Trish Iboshi, a devotee of hotel living at home, feels a twinge now and then. When I first talk with her, she is deeply smitten with the ultimate in domestic outsourcing: the dot-com delivery service. Sprouting up mainly in cities, these services deliver almost anything—a can of soda, a video, a housecleaner—often in less than an hour. They serve a crowd that loves doing business with a click, and usually has little clue about domestic life. (Iboshi especially swoons when a service sends an extra cookie with her order, or makes her bed in a snappy way.)

Iboshi subscribes to two services: one sends a weekly housecleaner to her Seattle home, picks up dry cleaning, delivers gifts, and dispatches a car mechanic and masseuse; another service delivers lunch to her office and last-minute food. She's ordered ice cream just before leaving her office, then driven home to meet the delivery truck. "I just didn't want to go to the store," she says petulantly. "I just wanted to go home. Any kind of service that's going to give me more time to relax and get my job done, that's good." This impulsiveness—the ability to be totally waited upon, at a whim—is, I sense, the attraction. That's why she draws the line at a grocery delivery service. "That's forcing me to think about what I buy," she says. "I'd even have to be home to let them in."

Asked about downsides to this way of life, she pauses. Maybe it is a sign that she's working too hard, she ventures. "Whatever happened to having a normal life, cooking a meal, having a family, and getting a dog? Whatever happened to having lunch with my dad every Wednesday? I do it, but not as much as I used to," she admits.

Still, when both of her services go bankrupt in the late nineties dot-com shake-out, Iboshi is heartbroken. For a time, she cleans her house, and one weekend she and her boyfriend even approach their garden. "We were going to pull weeds, but I didn't know a weed from a flower," she says. Now, she is betwixt and between, not terribly interested in learning these domestic chores but too time-pressed to find household help or a new delivery service on her own. "I have to find a gardener. Somebody just won't arrive tomorrow," she laments. "Before, it was all so easy."

Why should we try to keep all domestic industries under our own roofs at such disadvantage and expense?

The topic is timely, but the author is no twenty-first-century pundit. Ellen Richards, an MIT graduate and founder of the home economics movement, posed this question in 1904, at the dawn of our consumer society. A century later, it seems like a contradiction in terms to think of home economics as cutting edge. Yet early on, home economists such as Richards tackled some of the most thorny societal questions of their day. They saw themselves as part of the turn-of-century progressive reformers who fought urban poverty, child labor, and inhumane working conditions. By bringing science to daily living, home economists sought to fix the woes of industrialization, house by house. Home economics, they felt, could serve as a springboard for connecting the home to the larger world, even for liberating women from their domestic shackles.

Whatever happened? Home Ec now conjures up as fusty an image as Victorian domesticity, and brings back memories of misshapen sewing projects and lumpy cookies. No longer mandatory in all public schools, it's studied less and less at the university level as well. Nevertheless, the subject—now called Family and Consumer Science—is still taken by millions of American children of both sexes. Often, it's the only class most will ever take that focuses on home life.

So, what are they learning? Do children raised on McDonald's snicker as they learn baking recipes they'll never replicate in their own kitchens? Does Home Ec cling to the myth that this is a nation of breadwinner husbands and scouring wives, or do any home economists carry on the aims of their field's idealistic pioneers? Could they unexpectedly offer the beginnings of a new domesticity, fueled by a belief that homes do matter? I was surprised by what I found.

Leaning on a worn cupboard in her Home Ec classroom, Marae McGhee begins her fifth back-to-back class of the morning at Metuchen High School in New Jersey. In her hand, she holds a package of macaroni and cheese mix. She brushes back a lock of graying hair, and patiently explains the day's assignment in a voice softened by vestiges of a Carolina drawl. Her juniors are to compare cupcakes made from a mix, stovetop macaroni and cheese, and traditionally popped popcorn with microwave versions. On this balmy May day, the dozen students seem listless, but when Mrs. McGhee finishes speaking, they break into assigned groups and get right to work, grabbing aprons, spoons, and pans.

Nothing is made from scratch. Everything comes from a box. Yet chatting with the students, I soon understand why. One Botticelli-faced fourteen-year-old named Francesca, wearing silver nail polish and her wispy brown hair tucked in a bun, describes a typical evening at home, as her classmates measure and stir beside her. Mostly, Francesca eats cereal for dinner, or nukes frozen food. She can't recall a time when she and her three siblings didn't cobble together their own suppers—separately. Only on rare occasions does her mother, a computer programmer, announce a family dinner. Her father is mostly on-call to his job as a limo driver. "Dinner isn't a big thing in our house," says Francesca, munching popcorn as we talk. "We eat at all different times."

A shy, redheaded girl at the same table speaks up before the bell rings. She eats with her mom, while her dad watches television. "A few times, he's sat down with us," she ventures quietly. The stories are similar in the half-dozen classes I visit that day in Metuchen, a fairly well-off middle-class suburb, and in the classes I visit another day in the more mixed-income town of Redbank, on the New Jersey shore. From a quarter to more than a third of the eighty-odd kids I informally poll rarely or almost never eat dinner with a family member. Most are on their own, as well, for breakfast and snacks. They tell me that their schedules just don't coincide with whomever they live—parents, grandparents, siblings. When families do gather to eat, many watch television at the same time.

That's not surprising, given decades of research tracking the decline of the American dinner hour and the rise of latchkey children. One national study found a substantial gap in parents' and children's views of how often they eat meals together: 67 percent of working parents say they eat a meal with their child every day, while 45 percent of children report doing so. Meanwhile, the number of children ages five to twelve taking care of themselves for some part of the day nearly doubled from 1.8 million to 3.4 million in the 1980s, according to the University of Michigan's Institute for Social Research. Children are being left alone at earlier ages and for longer periods of time, teachers say.

No wonder baking cookies from scratch is out, and packaged mixes are in. A great deal of home economics teaching concerns latchkey survival skills, from finding the fuse box when the lights go out to fixing your own dinner at age twelve. Born into a society of instant food and breakneck schedules, Home Ec students are often being raised on nothing but instant food and breakneck schedules. One teacher told me children should learn how to turn off the water in an emergency, because often the parents don't know themselves. Not so long ago, Home Ec taught future housewives how to bake cupcakes they'd make for their future families. The new Home Ec teaches children how to cobble together some kind of home life—now.

*Home is no longer a haven, it's more akin to a
railroad station.*

Undoubtedly, children learn a great deal of
independence and self-reliance when they spend time
alone. "Around nine or ten, kids want to care for themselves
and don't want to be in programs for babies anymore,"
notes sociologist Sandra L. Hofferth. A study of thirty
middle-schoolers by University of Southern California
sociologist Elaine Bell Kaplan found that many children,
astutely seeing food as a symbol of caring, felt proud when
they helped out their families by cooking. Still, some felt
burdened by the chores they had to take on, and others
resented the loss of family dinners and the cooking of "real"
food.

When I spoke with children about spending time alone
at home, even those who felt that the experience ultimately
taught them independence primarily talked of their fear.
Not boredom or glee, but fear. They were afraid when they
were first left alone at ages five, six, and up, and some were
still afraid. Sixteen-year-old Ellen told how she ran and hid
in the upstairs bathroom one night when she thought she
heard an intruder. She was terrified, but her parents and
older siblings later teased her, saying it must have been the
wind. Eighteen-year-old Wesley used to be spooked by the
family's answering machine, which announced the time.
"The voice would echo through the house," he said, his eyes
wide at the memory.

David Elkind, author of *The Hurried Child*, calls family
life today "permeable," meaning it's open and vulnerable to
the complexity and diversity of post-modern society. Home
is no longer a haven, it's more akin to a railroad station—"a
noisy hub of activity that provides food, information and
transportation much more than it provides nurturance," he
writes. Schedules and lists are the currency of family
members' autonomous lives, replacing steady, regular
contracts—and contact—between parent and child.
Equipping kids with beepers and cell phones can be another
way to substitute busyness for true relations. Some
parenting and domesticity gurus even suggest applying

principles of business to the family. Kathy Peel advises families to adopt a mission statement, designate one parent the family manager, and mandate standard operating procedures for chores.

In this new world, children are considered competent and share authority with their parents. They're often expected to perform at levels that are age-inappropriate and stressful. One New Jersey teacher tells me she spends hours coaching eleven- and twelve-year-olds how to stay home alone, and how to talk to parents they rarely see. She warns kids not to bother grownups when they first get home from work, and tells them they're responsible for keeping their parents up-to-date with their school activities. "They don't realize parents have a life," she sighs.

The old ways of life weren't all wonderful. For most of the twentieth century, society wouldn't tolerate parents who didn't fit the traditional mold, or couldn't provide a safe haven for their young. The inner life of the home could be as violent as the outside world. But today the balance is tipped in the other direction, toward a home life that's hard on the young. Many children know almost nothing of domesticity, and their relations with others in the house is fleeting. For some children, a meal means taking a bowl of cereal and a spoon into their room, says Home Ec teacher Doris Cochran of Redbank.

In orphaning domesticity, we're throwing away a crucial chance to show that we care for one another.

Just as dusting or scrubbing doesn't automatically make a home, so dinner hours or after-school time with a grownup doesn't instantly create nurturing family relations. But these domestic chores and rituals are building blocks of relationships that, in turn, distinguish a railroad station from a home. We will continue to move toward what Professor Jagdish Sheth calls "roommate families" if we don't value ways of constructing and strengthening human relationships. "We'll have a household, not a home," says Sheth, a professor of marketing at Emory University. "We'll have shared living." In her study of middle-school children, Elaine Kaplan found that children who were always cared for, or those who received little care at all, grew up without knowing how to care for others. She concludes that caring, like academic competency, is a learned skill.

Quietly, home economics is offering children the barest underpinnings of a home life by teaching them skills they're learning nowhere else. Many teachers are trying to move away from the field's fatal turn toward sexism in the 1920s. At that time, the influence of a Long Island housewife named Christine Frederick steered home economics away from a focus on societal ills and toward the professionalization of household work. Working out of her home "experiment station," Frederick used efficiency principles borrowed from business, including stopwatch techniques that verged on the comic. (At least she was trying to apply business principles to housework, not family members, as many domestic gurus do today.) Yet while seeking to liberate women from their most onerous chores, she still believed they belonged at home. "Our greatest enemy is the woman with the career," she said in 1914. That attitude, naturally, became an albatross for home economics.

When I called to ask permission to visit Redbank High School, the jovial principal chuckled and said, "Home Economics? Now there's a dying breed!" That may be true. But if so, it's due not only to its sexist image but to our willingness as a society to denigrate home. Many women have hurried to run away from domestic life because, for so long, they were saddled with domestic work to the exclusion of most else in life. Although men increasingly take part in parenting their children, they stay away from picking up the fallen mantle of domesticity because it's been a demeaned realm for so long. Yet in orphaning domesticity, we're throwing away a crucial chance to show that we care for one another, to show that we're willing to spend time together in an increasingly hurried world.

Instead, we're trying to buy domestic lives as if they were boxes of macaroni and cheese. Even if paying strangers to do our dirty work buys us time to take our children to museums, is that how we want to teach them to live? Do we want to teach them that life is play to the exclusion of all else? For an article I wrote on Generation X in the workplace, a head buyer from Macy's told me that young trainees now want to go to the Giorgio Armani show, a plum assignment, in their first weeks on the job. Along with removing many chances for intimacy, outsourcing all domestic life is like showing children they only need to go to the Armani shows in life. "Why else have a house if you don't do your own work?" asked Ellen, the teen from Metuchen. "What's the point if you're not spending time in it and doing the chores? It's part of being a family."

Likewise, leaving children to fend for themselves too often teaches them to care only for themselves. One mother who works in public relations told me that she reassessed her busy life after her teenage daughter asked her one day, "Mom, why do we always have milk but no cereal, or cereal but no milk?" Sharing every meal isn't necessary in order to foster intimacy at home. But neither should family meals be such a low priority. Centuries ago, no one had to schedule family time, because people's lives revolved around working and playing with members of their households. In seventeenth-century Holland, a cradle of modern domesticity, even upper-class women washed, cooked, and mended alongside servants. In many pre-Victorian cultures, people sat down to formal meals mostly only on religious and civil holidays, and ate here and there on a daily basis. But now, when families don't work together and their days are often spent far apart, meals are an important opportunity for forging human connections. In an era when we make so few deep connections to others in society, it's crucial that we preserve home as a place where the young can find intimacy and a sense of belonging.

I don't want to wear that apron. I want to choose which parts of the world I inhabit. I want to earn my keep, and navigate a society larger than my kitchen. But I will also continue to make banana muffins, sit down to supper with my daughters as often as I can, and coax them to clear the table. Unless we all—men and women alike—care about domesticity, we may as well live in hotels, and pass our kin coming and going in the hallways, as if we're nothing more than strangers.

Diary: The Dinner Hour

We have tried all manner of dinner hours—children eating first, adults later; all the family around the table; short-order cooking for each family member.

At first, this experimenting did not stem from any great plan. When our daughters were very small, we just wanted to fill their tummies before they dozed off into their soup. Like many parents, we hoped to feed them the healthiest food we could muster in a hurry, and teach them to use their fork and spoon more than once in a while. Watching a baby dive into her first banana or lap up her beloved puréed squash was a joy. Catching a rare meal tête-à-tête with my husband was wonderful. But on the whole, dinner was a chaotic and unpredictable nightly chore.

At one point, our babysitter was feeding the girls their supper at 5 p.m., both because our littlest one went to bed by 7 p.m. and because my husband and I cared for my elderly mother after our work. Along with eating separately from mom and dad, the girls—then an infant and toddler—required different foods. As the years went by, however, this arrangement grew into short-order cooking. For lunch and dinner on weekdays, they got anything they requested from the sitter. I felt uneasy on weekends when they pouted if one didn't get pizza and the other scrambled eggs. We began thinking about a family dinner hour. We wanted to do more than make sure that four people somehow got fed each night.

We certainly weren't hankering after a Norman Rockwell scene, a re-creation of traditional family dinners of long ago. I grew up with supper on the table at 6 o'clock, since both my parents' jobs allowed them to be home each night. My husband's family had a "split shift," with his homemaker mom cooking an early dinner for the children, putting them to bed, then eating later with his dad. Our lives today couldn't be more different. Unfailing family traditions such as the nightly dinner hour are rare, and certainly not a daily occurrence. As our early experimenting showed, we were making up the rules as we went along. Who cooks when both parents work? How important are manners? Should we serve kid-friendly or more sophisticated foods? These questions are tough, but not impossible to answer. It takes work. Flexibility and experimenting needn't preclude constancy and custom.

So we began trying to eat dinner as often as possible together, and share one meal when we did. I knew instinctively that sharing the same food could combat the sort of spoiled-princess attitude that grew from short-order cooking. I also thought that we would be able to make more progress on manners if we, their parents, ate with them. Our babysitter had fed our daughters but hadn't shared the meal herself. So our girls didn't see a knife and fork in action very often. We had little more than these vague ideas when we set out to create our family dinner hour.

I have been surprised by what I've learned. In two years of eating together most but not all nights, I've discovered that manners and food are not that important. Certainly, sharing food teaches important life lessons in taking what comes your way, and appreciating what we have. Learning manners teaches our children a currency of thoughtfulness and care. We use a napkin to protect our clothes, to save on wear and washing, to preserve the planet, etc. We don't interrupt because we want to listen and we want to be heard. But most of all, manners enable us to help each other with the real task at hand each night: our conversation.

In these two years, I've discovered that the goal of the dinner hour is *not* seeing our children put their napkin in their laps, or polish off a pile of crisp green beans. The real joy of this time has been watching them grow proficient in the art of conversation. At first, they spoke only to one another at dinner, and only in a sort of babble of play. Now, we laugh and have fun, but we also explore the roller coaster of their school day, why a classmate is bossy, what we might do on our next vacation, even why China is scuffling diplomatically with the United States—all topics you cannot tackle on the fly.

It's still not easy. Milk spills, forks lie unused. Sometimes, the girls both speak so fast, words tumbling out, that they interrupt each other, then pout—each feeling that the fragile river of their thoughts was unjustly thwarted.

At other times, they relish our conversation so much that they are reluctant to leave the table. Then I realize that this sometimes haphazard dinner hour is an island, a verbal refuge for our family, a time when, amid the interruptions and busyness of daily life, we can connect for a few minutes of the day. It is a struggle to create and keep this dinner hour, and perhaps we'll never stop experimenting. But this is the kind of housework that creates a home.

TOWARD
A
NEW
VISION
OF
HOME

FOUR

Creating a Home at Work:

The Lure of the

New Company Town

I don't see this would ever replace my community at home. . . . Well, maybe the Monday-to-Friday community.

Kristen Thurber, employee

"Strawberry, blueberry, or chocolate chip?" Thor Johnson asks, spatula in hand as he prepares to flip another batch of flapjacks browning on the griddle.

It's almost 9 a.m. in the New York offices of e-commerce consultants Agency.com, and Johnson is energetically presiding over a monthly pancake breakfast for employees. The company doesn't open for another hour, yet about twenty-five people, many dressed in T-shirts and jeans, are gathered in the sleek kitchen, chatting in small groups. Johnson, head of Agency.com's New York office, cooks from a recipe displayed on his laptop, while keeping up a friendly banter with his staff. He jokes that the recipe is a family secret, then turns to bestow pancakes and praise on a worker for a job well done. "Thanks, I know that was a pain in the butt," Johnson says in a booming voice.

Down the hall is the company's Asian-inspired Zen Den, where employees can hang out or take a meditative moment to themselves. After hours, staff can receive biweekly massages or attend "InspireU," informal employee-taught classes on topics ranging from winetasting to aerobics. Up on the building's top floor, construction workers are unpacking a pool table in a bright new subsidized cafeteria with stunning views of the Statue of Liberty and New York Harbor.

It all looks like fun and games. But stepping away from the griddle, Johnson explains the rationale behind the perks. To begin with, creating a social life for employees helps foster teamwork and creativity. If a worker takes a break in the Zen Den, she's liable to get to know coworkers better, and perhaps they'll brainstorm. Taking a solo breather outside the office doesn't promote teamwork, says Johnson. A comfortable, social environment also keeps workers from jumping to a competitor. It all adds up to glue—the glue that binds the work community. "From a purely mercenary point of view, we're just trying to figure out ways to keep people in the office," says Johnson bluntly. "You don't want them to go home and play. You don't want them to go out to dinner with their pals. You want them here working," even if "work" is as loosely defined as a cheery pancake breakfast.

Johnson is a big, burly bear of a man, with a thatch of Nordic blond hair and a strong jaw. When he speaks, he commands attention. Excusing himself from our conversation for a moment, he chides the employees who are supposed to be watching the pancakes. "Okay flippers," he barks, half jokingly. "Someone is being negligent on that griddle!"

This morning of pancake flipping is very dot-com, as conscious a poke at the usual corporate stuffiness as wearing cutoffs and flip-flops to a client meeting. But in its own style, Agency.com is doing something quite mainstream. Employers from start-ups to Fortune 500s are offering dry cleaning, exercise, shopping, checkups, chaplains, and charitable work on the job. They're building elementary schools and napping rooms and holding poetry and Bible readings. Employees now turn to hotlines for advice on where to find an engagement ring, a plumber, or a nursing home for mother. They shop at their employer's "Main Street" or "Village," then return to work in office "neighborhoods." Some frills are axed when the economy slows, but the push remains—to create whole worlds at the office.

What happens to home when so much of life is lived at work?

But what happens to home when so much of life is lived at work? Perhaps depending on our employers for our fun and domestic life is just another way to outsource home chores. Along with hiring a slew of strangers to do domestic work, maybe we're foisting the challenge of daily living onto our employer's shoulders. Is this one-stop shopping for survival in a time-starved society? It's not that simple. Partaking of company services isn't as simple as exchanging money for a good, as Thor Johnson explained. Working out at the company health club is a complex transaction, particularly if the CEO hopes to see you in Sunday's three-mile race for the charity of his choice.

The new workplace is much more than a twentieth-century mall. It rekindles a grand social experiment of the past: the company town. These Industrial Age towns, home to more than two million people by 1930, foreshadowed the blurring of the lines between work and home we're experiencing today. Towns such as Pullman, Illinois, or Humphreysville, Connecticut, took "home" and transported it lock, stock, and barrel to company turf. Today, Information Age companies such as Agency.com are in many ways doing the same. This parallel between past and present makes me wonder what happened to the idea of home in company towns so long ago, and what happens when home is experienced at work today? Does a world of pancake breakfasts and poetry slams further erode the idea of the personal, private sanctuary we call home, or strengthen it by moving it to the place where Americans spend most of their time?

Throughout the history of the American company town, corporate beneficence had been traded for domestic freedom and privacy.

As we move into an era when physical boundaries are increasingly shattered by technology, this notion of the "mobile home" will grow more crucial. The company is just one in a number of places where we seek sanctuary these days. We look for home-like rooms when we vacation. We put our "dens" on wheels, transforming our cars into mobile media centers with TVs and laptop plugs. More and more, we seek the sanctuary of home on the move. Ultimately, this new way of life promises either an alluring new flexibility, a disturbing rootlessness—or perhaps both.

More than a century before Thor Johnson flipped pancakes for his staff, George Mortimer Pullman sought the best lifestyle for his workers. The scale of his vision, however, encompassed far more than pool tables and Zen Dens. In 1880, Pullman built an entire town—the grandest company town in American history—nine miles south of Chicago for the workers who manufactured his luxurious sleeper railcars.

With its wide boulevards, well-tended gardens, and Queen Anne-style buildings of red brick, the town of Pullman quickly became so famous that it ranked as one of Chicago's top tourist attractions. Weekend trains ran from the city so onlookers could gawk as the company built a luxury hotel, Market Hall, church, school, parks, and state-of-the-art worker houses fitted with gas and running water. The town's block-long arcade building boasted thirty shops, a bank, post office, library, and a theater.

Pullman spared little expense in building the town because he hoped to attract the best skilled workers to his railroad yards. But he also wanted more: to mold his workforce into a sober, productive lot, and to make sure it stayed that way. To that aim, the town was as rigidly controlled as it was beautiful. George Pullman chose the productions for the town theater to ensure their propriety. The company retained ownership of the housing; workers could only rent. Residents were reminded to dress properly, keep their houses clean, and refrain from hanging out on stoops. "In many ways, the people of Pullman were made to feel that they were on public display and must act so as not to shame the company," writes historian Stanley Buder. In Pullman, home life was not a private affair.

This was not new. Throughout the history of the American company town, corporate beneficence had been traded for domestic freedom and privacy. Eight decades before Pullman built his town on Lake Calumet, a friend of Thomas Jefferson's built a Connecticut mill village that was modest in scope yet as lofty in intention as Pullman's creation. Col. David Humphreys brought in orphan boys from New York to serve as worker-apprentices in his wool mill. Determined, like many American businessmen of his day, to avoid the horrible working conditions of Britain's "dark Satanic mills," Humphreys strictly regulated their bedtimes, churchgoing, and schooling. He even wrote the plays they performed on holidays. In Massachusetts, Francis Cabot Lowell provided a surrogate home for the local girls he hired to work in his early nineteenth-century textile mills. The strict rules in such mill boardinghouses— "a 10 p.m. curfew, required church attendance on Sunday, and the prohibition of smoking and gambling—mirrored the values that parents guarded in rural life," writes historian Tamara Hareven.

Other early American company towns followed a less Puritan, but equally tight-leashed model. While Lowell mill girls were paid in cash and smothered in rules, many Rhode Island workers weren't supervised after work, but were paid in chits at the company store, where a price hike meant an instant wage cut for the workers. In 1843, owner Benjamin Cozzens warned his workers in Crompton Mills that those who didn't buy from the company store "are informed that there are plenty of others who would be glad to take their places at less wages."

Some New England mill workers managed to grow their own food and livestock, and maintain a separate life from the factory. In 1829, Massachusetts mill agent N. B. Gordon complained in his diary that on Election Day he "could not peaceably work the mill as all hands seemed determined to have the whole day." Yet over the next two centuries, most company towns leaned more toward the paternalism of Humphreysville and Pullman.

The vast Amoskeag Corporation, which operated dozens of textile mills in Manchester, New Hampshire, between 1837 and 1936, owned at most fifteen percent of its workers' houses and provided only a modest array of educational and social programs. Yet Amoskeag workers still felt the company controlled their lives. "The Amoskeag was a continuation of the old feudal system, where the lord of the country, or whoever it was, took care of hundreds of people that worked for him or were connected with him," said mill worker Tommy Smith. "The attitude was there." By the 1920s, many Amoskeag workers had grown reluctant to participate in the company's extracurricular classes or clubs, preferring to center their lives around activities separate from work.

Relations between a worker and the boss are always complex. The relationship can be of mutual benefit: an employee gains a means of survival and an identity, while the employer profits, financially and from the psychological currency of power. Along with feeling discontent with the company's control, nineteenth- and twentieth-century workers were genuinely grateful for perks, such as housing that afforded them a toilet for the first time. "I felt like a millionaire—we didn't have to run outside," recalls Ernest Anderson, an Amoskeag worker. Some Pullman residents reveled in the town's ban on alcohol, thankful to leave behind the many saloons of the Chicago slums. Still in the end, it was Pullman, not the workers, who decided to ban drinking. It was the Amoskeag bosses who decided who got the mill work and company housing. So powerful and inescapable was Amoskeag in the city of Manchester that workers who were fired sometimes desperately disguised themselves in order to apply for another mill job. "It was either that or starve to death," said mill worker William Moul.

Eventually, such paternalism helped bring down the American company town. Chafing at the restrictions on their freedom and given new mobility by the automobile, many workers moved out, sometimes amid bitter labor battles that periodically crippled industry. Even Pullman's many amenities couldn't prevent discontent. In 1894, a bitter strike crippled the company and set off the slow decay of the beautiful model town. The strike had complex origins, yet not least was Pullman's inability to acknowledge his suffocating control of the town. Believing his roles as landlord and employer as separate, Pullman triggered the walkout by cutting wages, then refusing to lower rents. In doing so, he showed his workers that the company's best interests came first, both in work and at home.

It is the workplace where most people learn about themselves, find out which values are truly important, make friends, develop their networks, eat their lunch, give to charity, fall in love, discuss television and sports, and learn what's on the minds of other people.

Alan Wolfe *One Nation, After All*

It's a quiet December morning before Christmas, and architect John Henderson is showing me around the New York recording studio offices he designed and furnished a year ago. The space isn't quite akin to Lowell's company boardinghouse or Pullman's trim brick worker houses; no one lives here. Yet I wouldn't have guessed I was standing in a corporate workspace. "It's the anti-office," says Henderson, a slight man with a perpetually amused expression. "It was supposed to look like a college group house."

He walks past a seedy old piano—"I was just looking for a junker"—and into the heart of the space, a kitchen and living room topped by an enormous circular skylight. In this area, there's an old bentwood rocking chair, a distressed country kitchen table, and a 1950s-style stove and fridge inspired by the "I Love Lucy" show. Nearly every piece of furniture is vintage, and many were purchased by Henderson at a props supply store. Surrounding the communal space are private offices, each decorated to the occupant's wishes. The company hasn't created an office in the heart of Manhattan. It's built a home.

This is the physical expression of the new company town—the more homelike, the better. The designers at Studios Architecture, where Henderson works, are finding more and more clients want to scrap the typical, corporate-issue furniture they've been buying for decades. Instead, they opt for pieces from varied manufacturers so their offices will look more eclectic and lived-in. In an enormous break from the past, Studios even buys residential furniture for corporate projects. Studios clients are cutting edge, and include many high-tech firms. But across the country, even staid corporations—Xerox, Owens Corning, Alcoa—are swapping private offices for open floor plans, punctuated by cafés—don't call them coffee shops!—and kitchens.

Recognizing these changes, office furniture maker Herman Miller enlisted a young Turkish industrial designer to create a new system of office furniture. In effect, Ayse Birsel was asked to redo the cubicle invented by Herman Miller designer, Bob Propst, in 1958. It was a heady assignment: design a twenty-first-century version of the workspace that has come to epitomize the grayness of corporate life. In its place, Birsel offers an office with flowing lines, quirky details, and enormous flexibility. Instead of placing workers in connected cubicle boxes, she places three workspaces in a circle, divided by movable cloth panels attached to a central pole. Petal-shaped roofs shelter the work areas, which sport bud vases and "porch lights." Unlike the recording studios' living room, you couldn't mistake Birsel's "Resolve" office for your den. Yet once again, the elements of home are being pulled into work.

> Yet an office can't become a home, since it
> doesn't belong to you.

"I don't think the office should be more like a home— per se," says Birsel, a svelte woman with jet-black hair who offers me a cup of strong coffee as we chat one winter's day. She herself is wrestling with the puzzle of where home fits into the new workplace she's studied for years. By incorporating a porch light into her design, she consciously borrowed a symbol of home. By allowing the cloth dividers to be easily changed, she allows people to customize their workspaces. "We wanted to create something that you could make your own," says Birsel, who is based in New York. "In a way, it becomes your home." Yet an office can't become a home, since it doesn't belong to you, asserts Birsel. As elegant and serene as a cat, she has a childlike joy in exploring these questions. Is she right, I wonder. Is it all that simple?

Such changes in office design reflect the new character of work in the information-fueled service economy: it's more communal, creative, fast-paced. But it's interesting that the stage is being set for this new work with icons borrowed from the domestic world—the porch light, kitchen, rocking chair. Increasingly, the physical manifestations of home are being imported to work.

What's more, the emotional life of home is following suit. As the lines fade between home and work, our innermost thoughts, our spiritual lives, and our social connections are increasingly ending up in the office. Nowhere is this trend more apparent than in the evolving role of the manager from corporate drill sergeant to a combination of nanny, therapist, and coach—a job description Kate Swann knows well.

A petite thirty-seven-year-old with an elfin face, Swann directs the New York office of Organic, a web marketing and design firm. As well as keeping up with the fast-paced Internet, Swann spends an enormous amount of time dealing with the social and emotional lives of her employees. Since material on the Internet can always be improved, the company's workload is theoretically endless. So Swann keeps a close eye out for designers and engineers who are burning out, then steps in to point out the need for balance. "We literally go around and if we see that people are, you know, spending the night in the office and stuff like that, we say to them, 'Go home. Take some time off!'" says Swann.

Swann talks in the youthful jargon of her staff, her speech sprinkled with "you know" and "like," and yet she sounds very much like a weary surrogate parent to her employees. When Swann learned that her workers felt their parents didn't understand their work, she hastily arranged a "Parents Day" so relatives could see in person that their offspring had respectable jobs. I suggest that she's more like a den mother than a typical manager, and she laughs but agrees.

Swann's concern isn't just altruism, of course. Like George Pullman or Thor Johnson, she wants to keep her employees happy to ensure that they stay and do good work for her. But she seems genuinely stunned at how much employees want from their company. "They always want more," she sighs. Organic's workers decorate their bathrooms and stop by the office on weekends, sometimes to hang out and sometimes to use the space for clubs that have nothing to do with work. Two programs that Swann says resemble therapy are extremely popular: coaching for managers and "facilitations" for employees. "They beg to get in," she says. Although the company provides free massages and twice-weekly yoga classes in-house, along with discounts to a gym in the same office building, the staff petitioned Swann for their own gym. "We're, like, there's one downstairs!" she protests.

Swann loves the informal atmosphere of the new workplace, where she can direct the company in a T-shirt and flowing skirt. She enjoys the camaraderie that springs from working long hours side by side, with breaks for pizza or bagels. Yet she's puzzled by her underlings' desire to bring just about everything that's personal, private, or domestic into the office. She is careful to draw some lines. "I personally would not go to yoga at work," she says, with a grin. "I don't necessarily need to have people see me with my bum in the air, all kind of sweaty and flushed! But people are really into it."

Why shouldn't workers love freebies, perks, and conveniences? I've spent my career in bare-bones newsrooms, working from gray cubicles that have never reminded me of home. Some benefits have been outstanding—five weeks of vacation in London per local custom, an eighteen-month unpaid maternity leave in New York. I've made lasting friends through work, and met my husband across the newsroom. Who's to say, then, I wouldn't snatch up the benefits Kate Swann offers, and then beg for more?

One reason employees seek the comforts of home at work is because they feel pressed for time. With Americans working an average of forty-four hours a week, most people spend the majority of their waking hours at the workplace.

Shifting the chores and even the social life of home to the office seems like a godsend. I recall discussing this issue with an executive secretary in San Antonio, Texas, who routinely works twelve-hour days at a big insurance company. Kathy Nusbaum is a single mother, so has precious little time for shopping, cooking, or cleaning. She frequents the more costly dry cleaner at work because others are closed by the time her workday ends. Several times a week, she confessed reluctantly, she takes packaged cafeteria dinners home for her teenage son. "If I didn't have access to all these niceties, I really don't know how I'd get these things done," she said.

As workloads have burgeoned, neighborhood and community ties have frayed. Certainly, local communities aren't dead. Americans on average belong to three or more organizations, such as churches or book clubs. Yet there has been a dramatic shift in our ties to neighbors and friends, according to research by Harvard professor Robert D. Putnam, author of *Bowling Alone: The Collapse and Revival of American Community*. How many people belong to an Elks Club or a Masonic Lodge these days? In the mid-1970s, the average American attended some club meeting every month, but by 1998, that attendance fell nearly sixty percent, Putnam found. How many neighbors do you know? Only twenty percent of people socialize with neighbors several times a week, down from thirty percent in 1974. "It's almost as if we set up our own islands," one suburban woman told Boston University professor Alan Wolfe. "It's a street full of islands. And you know, we would love to have a great relationship and great neighbors and that sort of thing, but it has just never evolved."

Instead of calling over the back fence for the name of a good electrician, people today are more likely to ask a workmate or an employee hotline. Once while visiting a large work-family consulting firm, I was taken into a room lined from ceiling to floor with open shelves that looked like mail slots. Each was filled with advice sheets for clients' employees. One sheet dispensed tips on toilet-training a toddler. Others told how to entertain your child in the car, or choose a nursing home for an aged parent. Now, time-pressed workers needn't do anything more than log on to their computer or dial the phone, anonymously of course, to get help on the most private family matters.

Depending on the company for help erodes priceless relationships.

My heart sank as I looked around. The tip sheets seemed so clinical and cold, piled in a gray, windowless room. Dispensing advice this way is no doubt fast and efficient, in keeping with the priorities of the Information Age. But depending on the company for help erodes priceless relationships—the chance neighborhood encounters that grow into friendships, the comfortable banter with the owner of the corner store, the family ties that ebb and flow but endure in times of anger or joy. During a walk in my neighborhood, I recently ran into a fellow mom who gave me a crumpled flier on children's language classes. Knowing my interest, she'd been carrying it around for weeks, hoping to bump into me. When an elderly neighbor hurt his hand, we made dinner for him and he thanked us with tickets to a chorus concert in which he sang. Such encounters are as important to the idea of home as privacy of space or domestic rituals. They make up the galaxy of relations that support a home.

It's a blue-sky Minnesota summer day, and Kristen Thurber is hobbling to her company's post office on a bandaged ankle broken on a family canoe trip. She's taking a break from her work as a technology manager at law publisher West Group to mail some letters. On the company corridor dubbed "Main Street," Thurber can also stop for coffee, shop for a birthday card, or pick up her dry cleaning. After finishing her errands, Thurber talks with me about her ties to work, and to family and friends. Smiling, she insists that her life outside of the office counts just as much her work world—at least on weekends. A minute later, I ask what else she'd like West Group to provide for employees, and she's quick to answer. "A gallon of milk, eggs," she smiles. "That would be nice."

A few tip sheets, a gallon of milk from the company store—these alone won't corrode the age-old web of human relations that surround a home. It's difficult to know exactly what role the corporation is playing in the complex dynamics between worker, community, and workplace. Nevertheless, importing the furnishings, chores, and emotions of home to the workplace makes it easier to depend on the company to solve the problems of life, big and small.

A day after visiting Kristen Thurber, I chat with Becky O'Grady, a rising General Mills executive who seems as wholesome as the cereals she helps produce. Tall, blond, and perky, she doesn't even try to argue that she has a life outside the sprawling company that locals fondly call "Generous Mills." She does her dry cleaning, car tune-ups, film developing, exercise, and more along the company's labyrinthine corridors. When not at work, she socializes almost entirely with workmates. In 1990, O'Grady was one of thirty MBAs recruited to join the company. Of that "class," six ended up marrying each other, including O'Grady and her spouse. "We've made a whole life here," she says with a grin, hugging a sheath of papers like a schoolgirl with a notebook.

Nobody regards Pullman as a real home, and, in fact, it can be scarcely said that there are more than temporary residents at Pullman.

Richard Ely, *Harper's Monthly*, 1885

Becky O'Grady doesn't live in a company boardinghouse, nor is she forced to shop at the company store or worship in her employers' church. She has the freedom of choice to work where she wants, and of course she may live where she chooses. The give-and-take between leaders and workers today doesn't compare with the autocratic power of bosses long ago. That's a crucial difference between the red brick town carefully crafted and ruled by George Pullman and the team-oriented, café-crowded workplaces of today.

Still, while twenty-first-century employees have more of a say, the company retains the last word. It's still dangerous to joke too freely with the boss, even if you're out climbing mountains during a team-building retreat. Relations with peers at work are ultimately instrumental. That means that relationships on the job, whether friendly or purely businesslike, have another side to them. A friend across the cubicle wall might pass on a great tip on finding a Florida condo, but hold back gossip on the job opening in accounts.

My morning at the pancake breakfast illustrates how power underscores relations at work—whether employees recognize it or not. One employee, who coached Agency.com's softball team and did volunteer work arranged by the company, praised Agency's efforts to get employees together socially, saying the events gave workers a needed break. Moments later, I stood chatting with a vice president who had a different take on the morning. "I'm not so sure the purpose of these activities is to relax," she said. "It's to foster community." In the first private moment I had with Thor Johnson, he immediately talked about discipline. "I'm trying to change the culture—start getting them to be accountable," he said quietly. "The first time we did this, people showed up at 9:01 a.m., and there were no pancakes." Three views on the pancake breakfast, and all valid. But Thor Johnson had the power to set the priorities, and make sure they were met. Amid the fun, it's increasingly easy to lose sight of the corporate power structure. As author Laura Nash points out, such corporate programs are intended to express care for employees. Yet this care, it's important to remember, is conditional on economic performance.

Compared with the paternalistic Industrial Age workplace, the new corporation is softer and gentler—a "nanny" in Nash's words. Yet companies today reach just as deeply into employees' private lives, from friendships to child care. This is not to say that the new workplace is Orwellian. Yet when the lines between home and work fade, management and employees alike begin to tread new ground. Workers give their whole selves to work—a tradeoff they don't always realize they're making. Bosses become more deeply involved in the management of personal lives than perhaps they bargain for.

Power underscores relations at work.

Not too long ago, Bank of America's management set up a new employee program called "Adopt an ATM" that asked employee volunteers to look after one of the company's ten thousand automated teller machines—on their own time and without pay. More than 2,800 of the bank's 158,900 workers signed up. "We thought it was a great idea," said an executive vice president at the bank. But the bank quickly scrapped the program after a California state labor commissioner stepped in, saying that unless the employees were paid, the program would violate wage and hour laws. In the end, the company instead set up a toll-free number that employees could call if they noticed problems at ATMs.

The "Adopt an ATM" episode seems like a simple pay dispute. Yet it illustrates how—once again—a company's interests come first, even in an age of team-building and creative work. In the end, the boss will get the last word on both foosball and weekend workloads. That makes workplaces today, beneath the fun, more akin to Pullman, Illinois, than we perhaps want to admit.

Although the town of Pullman boasted the very best in worker housing and the most grand community buildings, residents did not tend to stay long. Worker housing remained filled, but residents spent a little more than four years on average in the town, according to an 1892 company census, one of many taken by Pullman. Workers moved out, swelling surrounding villages and commuting to the company railyards, partly because company housing could only be rented, not owned. But, they also moved out because the company cast a long shadow over life in Pullman. The average worker had almost no say in local government: only one town body was elected—the school board. When Richard Ely, a Johns Hopkins University economics professor on assignment for *Harper's Monthly*, asked a resident in 1885 if this transience turned the town into one big hotel, she amended him. "We call it camping out," she said.

These words of a century ago recall the observations of designer Ayse Birsel. You can't make a home at work, since it will never belong to you, she said. The fatal flaw of Pullman, Illinois, was that workers never felt as though it belonged to them. They had a roof over their heads, but never had homes to call their own. Their houses—governed by company rules, owned by the firm, watched by management—were false homes, and residents knew it. Yet isn't that, in a sense, what we're creating today when we turn to our employers to solve our life's problems, big and small? A "home" at work is out of our control, lacking in privacy, and hardly a sanctuary.

The company towns of long ago thrived in large part because they were islands, where management could control just about every aspect of public and private life. They died off when workers could drive down the road to avoid the company store or to find a new job. Today, we have endless mobility as the barriers of geography and time fade away. We can make friends across the globe via the Internet, and become world consumers and workers. Paradoxically, this is just when many of us are seeking a sense of belonging and feeling of home at work. We're searching for roots in a place we can never truly "own." If we continue on this path, we're creating homes just as false as the housing of Pullman.

It would be wrong to ignore the wonders of the new workplace, which benefit both company and employee. I'd be happy to help rake the gravel in a Zen Den, or mail my Christmas packages at work. Many of the current changes in the workplace reflect the economy's enormous shift from an industrial to a service base, from a workforce making widgits to one designing web pages. As work up and down the corporate ladder has changed, many more people have creative jobs that demand fast thinking and more of their whole selves. This removes the lines that rigidly divided the sides of ourselves we once reserved for "work" and "play."

We all need to keep a place that's purely our own.

But there's a big difference between making work more homelike to accommodate these changes on the job—and trying to make a home at work. If we're bringing our whole selves to our work, it's even more important to make a strong home outside the office where we can recharge. We needn't re-create the impermeable boundaries between work and home forged in the Industrial Age. Each person's boundaries will be drawn differently. I might come for a pancake breakfast, but shun the office yoga class. You might play on the company softball team, but skip the beer bash so you can be home for dinner. But we all need to keep a place that's purely our own, where relationships are not ruled by economics, where humanity trumps profits.

Keeping a strong home alive outside work means that the new workplace becomes a vibrant extension, not a replacement, of our neighborhood and community. In this era, we not only carry our work with us day-to-day, but change jobs far more often than our fathers and grandfathers did. If we grow too dependent upon our workplace, a change in job may mean losing, or at the least shaking up, important social supports—friendships, trusted doctors, our children's ties to caregivers. But when we have a home to call our own, we have the ability to be flexible, knowing our mobility is grounded. Building our own homes, in effect, sets us free. Living at work is a kind of permanent exile.

Diary: A Place to Work

Recently, I went back to the borrowed office where I started the journey of writing this book. I had spent a month there in November and early December, panic-stricken by the self-imposed deadline of finishing a chapter by the time we went away for Christmas. Since then, I had not returned.

I had been so adamant that I'd needed a separate office. Having "an office" would validate my crawl-out-on-a-limb decision to take a leave and write this book. Having a place to commute to would help me draw the lines between work and home, just as I did in my job. The room offered by a friend with an antiques business seemed just the ticket, a high-ceilinged room with a big window overlooking a leafy tree. I had thought it would be simple to transfer life from the office—where my company set up the computer and kept it running, supplied the pencils and the water fountain—to this bright, new workspace.

But my new office couldn't fill those big shoes. Sometimes, the antiques showroom closed and I wanted to work on. I tried coffee shops, but that option soon lost its luster. Nor was I sure where to keep my growing stacks of papers and files. It became apparent that I needed to decide which workspot ranked as my primary office, and which was a temporary daytime perch. Gradually, I stopped going to this dream office and stayed in my bedroom to work.

I had wanted an office apart from my home so badly that I hadn't realized that separating work and home wasn't just a matter of getting out of the house to work. I had forgotten the routines, culture, equipment, and networks that make up a "workspace." Those aren't easily transferred at the flick of a laptop or cell phone switch.

Certainly, one day we may be able to set up an office anywhere. Work is becoming more portable in this new Internet Age. We can do snatches of work during traffic jams, or chatter on cell phones as we drive—at the risk of driving like drunks, of course. We can digitalize our phone lists and engagement calendars, e-mail from anywhere, or hunt down each other on boats, planes, or trains.

But my transition from "mama corporation" to temporary office to bedroom-workroom made me realize the importance of carving out a "place" to work in this mobile society, a process that, like a relationship, takes time and effort. True mobility isn't yet possible because we are still attached to the physicality of colleagues, of papers, of work. We need routines to help us get going in the morning, and we need the familiarity of social relations, even if it's only saying hello to the cat in passing. Road warriors end up turning their car, spare bedroom, or local coffee shop into a base camp in order to function.

I learned something more. I had wanted so badly to keep a strong boundary between work and home that I didn't recognize that actually I had been keeping a gulf between these two worlds. Now, I'm beginning to realize that it's possible to draw and redraw, cross and re-cross that line day by day, yet still respect the boundary.

This morning, my four-year-old said, "Why don't you come back before my nap, so you can give me a kiss?" By coming back, she meant come out of my bedroom-office. Ten months ago, she would have cried if I had visited with her at midday. Now she was asking me to integrate myself in her day, then step back to the world of work.

Certainly, negotiating these boundaries is difficult. I've spent many moments sneaking out of the kitchen for a cup of tea when my little one is napping, or planning my entrances and exits to my children's time away from home. Sometimes, I'm so desperate to get out of my bedroom that I read a book in the library when I should have been home making phone calls. I've spent an entire walk across the park talking on the cell phone, while hushing my daughter's peeps from the stroller. I'm not always proud of the way I integrate home and work. It's just as possible to miss out on home when you work at home, as when you commute to an office.

Tearing down that gulf between home and work demands constant adjustments large and small, whether you're a young web designer, a crazed investment banker, or a part-time working mom. We have to make up the rules, step by step, often alone. But I'm learning to like many things about my new life. I've learned not to chastise myself for running to the store during the middle of the day to replace my daughter's lost camp swim goggles. Ten months ago, I would have sat puritanically in the office rather than taint my workday with that chore, even if I really had a light workload.

Now I emerge from the bedroom when I hear a voice that melts my heart, and I spend ten minutes watching the little one chomp her peanut-butter-and-jelly sandwich like a puppy relishing its dinner—all over the face, too much in the mouth, all enjoyment. Then I tell her that I'll soon go back to work and she'll take her nap. Or I take a few minutes to chat with my giggling second-grader and her freckle-faced friend as they dress their dolls in the lofty lair of a top bunk. I cross and re-cross the divide between home and work less fearfully and with more assurance.

Where I work—in a corner of my home—is for now the physical representation of how I work. I don't barricade myself in my home office and stonily will myself to slog through eight hours for good or naught. I open the door and allow life to intrude on my work. I'm learning how to let myself have a life just outside my office door.

FIVE

Home-ing:

Domestic Moves
in Search of Refuge

I'm not trying to have a permanent home. I want the flexibility.

> Bill McNish, a businessman who
> commutes between two Michigan
> homes

New Yorkers, like Parisians, pack their bags and go away in August. Restaurant reservations and subway seats are easy to get as the pace of the metropolis slows and the weather grows sticky. We often stay put in the city, enjoying its emptiness. But one summer, circumstances led us to try a twist on this ritual: we moved from apartment to apartment within New York. This nomadic existence proved both exhausting and exciting, and taught me a great deal about home.

Our journey began when the 1928 plumbing in our two bathrooms started to leak on the neighbors below. We timed the repairs for our vacation, expecting that when we returned, at least one toilet would work. But when we arrived home one languid evening—with a carsick daughter throwing up just steps from our building, as if to express her homesickness—the apartment was uninhabitable. A bathtub and lengths of piping sat in the front hall. The bathrooms were rubble. We retreated to the apartment of an understanding friend who was out of town—the first of three city homes we ultimately borrowed from vacationing friends as our renovations stretched far beyond a promised five weeks.

My husband and I, both former foreign correspondents who love travel, found it fun to camp in these apartments. We felt strange opening cupboards or drawers looking for spoons or towels, and after a while, we tired of sleeping in different beds. Nevertheless, we made ourselves at home, eagerly exploring new neighborhoods and relishing new views of the city from each apartment's windows. Our daughters carted favorite dolls from house to house, and I set up my laptop in two dining rooms, a kitchen, and a home office. We returned home to pick up mail and telephone messages, or use our printer. It was difficult, but liberating. Just as work had become a portable exercise, so we were experimenting with a new kind of mobile living.

Later, it occurred to me that our summer of domestic moves echoed a collective American search for "home" outside home. In an age when technology weakens physical boundaries, Americans are paradoxically seeking out and setting up "homes" wherever they go. A friend in Denver reads his Sunday paper, not in his own house, but in a nearby Starbucks, a generic living room where strangers hang out without speaking to one another. The middle- and upper-classes are passing on rustic summer cottages in favor of comfortable second houses where they both work and play all year-round. On vacation trips, Americans seek home-like hotel rooms with kitchens, or all manner of timeshare arrangements. At a time when people commonly speak of living in their cars, the lines between mobile homes and automobiles are blurring. One new car can be turned into a sporty camper; "think of it as 'Road Warrior' without the weaponry," comments an auto writer. A concept minivan comes with refrigerator, washer/dryer, vacuum, and microwave—to some consumers' chagrin.

My experiment with mobile living came to an end, and I own neither a car nor a second home. Still, I wonder whether my experience and our larger search for other homes reflect a push for a more flexible, perhaps portable home—or a slide into homelessness? Are we searching for home because we've ruined the sanctity of our primary abode? Perhaps in the Internet Age, we will break free from the tethers of place, particularly the sometimes suffocating ties that bind us to one home. But will we be able to make a place of sanctuary—in effect, a home—anywhere we go?

These are not all new questions. Once upon a time, the invention of the railroad, the steamship, and the automobile made travel universal and seemingly constant. "The tendency of the times is to render men homeless in more than the material sense," wrote Anna McClure Sholl in 1906. In an *Atlantic Monthly* essay entitled "The House," she argued that when the rich divide their time between homes "there is no time for . . . those accumulated impressions which make up the sense of home." For the masses, in turn, "home is the tent, the lodging house, the vestibuled car, the ocean steamer, the furnished house to rent for a season." As an antidote to this rootlessness, Sholl didn't explicitly mention the cult of domesticity, yet she lauded an equally rigid ideal—an ancient homestead, shaped by generations of the same family. Sholl did not see home and mobility comfortably coexisting.

That's our challenge in the twenty-first century. In an age when mobility and technology dilute the importance of place, we need to create a more flexible idea of home. The difficulty lies in redefining home in ways that allow us to preserve—or in many cases, restore—the comforts of homes past, without losing the flexibility and freedom the Information Age potentially gives us. The question becomes: can we find sanctuary, privacy, and intimacy only in our primary homes, or could we make a home in "the tent, the lodging house, the vestibuled car . . ."? Where do we want to be at home?

We need to create a more flexible idea of home.

Turn off the freeway between Detroit and Chicago, just before you hit Indiana, and you'll come to the tiny town of New Buffalo, Michigan. Cross the railroad tracks, with the vast blue waters of Lake Michigan stretching before you, then you'll find yourself on a wide main street that resembles a movie set for an old Western. A few of the low brick and wood-shingle shops are shabby and, on this October day, some have hand-lettered signs saying, "Closed Until Spring." In better-kept boutiques, a children's sweater sells for $90, and a butter-soft suede women's jacket carries a $500 price tag. New Buffalo—not so long ago a down-on-its-heels summer mecca—is in transition, a town being transformed by Chicagoans seeking second homes.

"It used to be that the restaurants all closed up after New Year's and reopened in the early spring. Now they're year-round," says realtor Gail Lowrie, who moved to the area from Chicago a decade ago after owning a weekend house in New Buffalo for years.

Lowrie nibbles at a salad as we sit in the sunny garden of an Italian restaurant, talking about second homes. A calm, motherly woman with an assured manner, she just changed jobs, joining the newly opened local branch of a large Chicago agency that's seeking to capitalize on the growing second home market. Congratulatory bouquets from an opening party the night before fill the swank agency, one of at least a half dozen in town. Although the lake waters are frigid and winter looms, Lowrie's day is filled with appointments. Some people say the town is turning into another suburb of Chicago, just an hour and fifteen minutes down the road. New Buffalo is hot.

But then again so are Branson, Missouri, Sanibel Island, Florida, and other little lake and seaside towns across the country. Although only about six percent of homes sold each year are second homes, sales in this area shot up nearly thirty percent nationwide in just five years. Undoubtedly, the booming 1990s stock market and healthy economy helped drive the rate of sales. But the boom doesn't tell the whole story. Long an idyllic symbol of summertime, the second home is becoming a more obligatory piece of the American Dream. Nearly one in three families believe that their chances of buying a second home are 50-50 or better, up from one in six families a decade ago. In contrast to previous generations, the trend seems to cross age groups. Interest in second homes is highest among adults younger than thirty-five.

Nor do buyers want Grandma's old cottage, with its chilly outdoor shower or rough-hewn weathered walls.

Today, the second homeowner might desire a wraparound porch or wooden floors, but seeks only the veneer of rusticity. Gail Lowrie describes new buyers as wanting "all the bells and whistles. The idea that you wouldn't have a garbage disposal or dishwasher is out of the question."

After lunch, she takes me for a drive along the lake, where multi-million dollar homes have been stuck on small plots next to older cottages with names like "Nothing Dune" or "Sans Souci." Along the quiet road, an inconspicuous ranch house neighbors a bright-white stucco mansion with Aegean blue trim. A stone Provencal-style manor dwarfs a bungalow. Every few hundred yards, a hive of construction crews swarm about a renovation or a new mansion born from a cottage's rubble. We stop at one torn-up property, where Lowrie introduces me to the owner, who has taken a tiny cottage and tripled it in size with a ballooning addition. The cozy, wood-paneled cottage, now a "guest wing," connects to a soaring living room, open kitchen, and enormous master bedroom suite with hefty Jacuzzi. As I leave, workmen are finishing what looks to be a cement-block fountain in the driveway.

Again, look past the excesses born from a robust age, and past a status-symbol mentality that is timeless. Look deeper and you'll discover a great deal about people's changing attitudes toward home. In generations past, cottages were opened with great ritual once or perhaps a few times a year, mostly in the summertime. E. B. White captured the rarity of such times, describing his family's annual trip to a rented lakeside cottage in Maine:

> The arriving (at the beginning of August) had been so big a business in itself, at the railway station the farm wagon drawn up, the first smell of the pine-laden air, the first glimpse of the smiling farmer, and the great importance of the trunks and your father's enormous authority in such matters, and the feel of the wagon under you for the long ten-mile haul, and at the top of the last long hill catching the first view of the lake after eleven months of not seeing this cherished body of water.

A half century later, Amy Willard Cross recalls in her book *The Summer House* taking a seventeen-hour train ride, an hour's drive, an overnight stay, a three-hour drive, a ferry ride, and finally a half-hour's drive each summer to get to her family's vacation cottage. No wonder such houses were idealized. They represented a pure, rare escape into the woods or to the shore.

In this century, rustic cottages still exist. But second homeowners more often trek in all seasons to a house as comfortable as their first. They're dividing life between two (and sometimes three) homes in a way that only the very wealthiest had in previous centuries. Aided by technology, they prolong weekend visits into habitual half-week stays— and work from their "vacation" homes. They spend major holidays such as Thanksgiving or Christmas in these homes. Perhaps most telling of their loyalties, many homeowners are waging legal battles for the right to have a say in the governance of their second communities. They're truly living in two places. Are such homes interchangeable or does each fulfill a different role in life? How does this mobility change the experience of home?

Our time here will be more personal time,
thoughtful time, and I would associate that
with home in the more classic sense.

Criss Henderson

The day after meeting Gail Lowrie, I drive along the old Red Arrow Highway hugging the lake to get to the second home of Rick Boynton and Criss Henderson. Off the two-lane highway, a winding road takes me into the hills, and deep into rain-washed woods turning tawny and rust. The house, painted an earth brown, nestles into a small valley, giving the sensation from within that you're in a treehouse.

The couple purchased the house only a week before, but seems completely at home. Pictures hang on the walls, and comfortable couches are neatly arranged in a two-story living room where enormous windows look out on the trees. At another end of the room, a wide dining table is decorated with a pair of candlesticks, and laid with warm blueberry muffins, sliced honeydew melon, and coffee. Boynton, a boyish, bespectacled man wearing a red baseball cap, butters a muffin as Henderson fixes a cup of tea. With classical music playing and three golden dogs sprawled about contentedly, the house looks well-settled.

The week, however, has not been entirely peaceful. Moving exertions aside, Boynton and Henderson were constantly interrupted by their work as leaders of Chicago's Shakespeare Theater. "The phones rang all week," says Henderson, a reserved man with an angular face and raven hair. "If the beepers weren't going, the phones were going, the faxes were going." At a first, more suburban house they'd owned in the area, they had tried to exclude work. They had deliberately not brought in a fax machine. But they concluded that these attempts at complete isolation were unrealistic. Since they now hope to spend more time in Michigan than ever before, they must find a way to keep connected to work while still trying to preserve the retreat that a second home represents to them. "We really want this to be a place of relaxation, but be realistic that we might have to work," says Boynton.

More and more, they feel that a second home is their only chance for retreat. They love their work, but it engulfs them night and day in Chicago, since the business and art of running the theater starts in the morning and ends late at night. Weekends are their busiest days, with the most shows. Although their city condo is as close to Lake Michigan as their country house is, they never stroll on the beach in the city. "We just give up trying to control work at home," says Henderson, sipping his coffee and gazing into the woods. "We don't even think about it. We don't even try." Their second home—where they have candlelit dinners, play music, savor the passage of time—is an escape from their first home.

This idea repeatedly arose in my interviews with more than a dozen second homeowners around the country. With technology and work invading the sanctity of the primary home, many people feel as if they can no longer control their lives there. As researcher Christena Nippert-Eng notes, when work and home are integrated, people spend a great deal of energy making and remaking boundaries. These days, the pace of non-work activities further squeezes out quiet moments, intimate relations, and time for thought. As a result, second homeowners often transfer the traditional domestic function of "retreat" to their alternative home. Nearly all the thirty British couples with second homes in France interviewed by researcher Davina Chaplin said that their homes no longer feel like a private enclave, due to the intrusions of work or the pace of urban living. "The first home had become merely a dwelling place with no other significance except its function as shelter," Chaplin writes.

How then do people preserve the second home as a retreat? Often, they use a seemingly immutable boundary, a demarcation that can't be erased by societal pressures, work demands, accelerating technologies: landscape. This natural boundary allows people to make their second homes into the retreats they've lost in their primary abodes. The second home may not be an unadulterated escape, but the idea of sanctuary is nevertheless paramount. Repeatedly, second homeowners, such as Florida entrepreneur Leslie Wolff, told me that a natural setting drew them back from work and worries, and helped break the increasing expectation that they should be always on-call.

"It's hard to find a place where you totally get away from it all," says Wolff. "When I am getting my e-mail and I'm in my bathing suit, I feel good. At least I'm in a mindset of relaxing and I'm more laid-back about returning a call or an e-mail." Wolff is anchoring herself to the landscape at a time when physical boundaries are being dissolved by technology and new ways to work.

For many, the journey to the second home helps separate a frantic daily life from a more leisurely pace by woods or shore. Rick Boynton and Criss Henderson relish the seventy-minute drive from Chicago to New Buffalo. To get to their house, they must cross through Chicago's urban sprawl, the industrial landscape of Gary, Indiana, then the farm country around New Buffalo. In doing so, they cross two state lines and the boundary between Central and Eastern time. Although they and most other visitors to the area keep their watches on Chicago time while in Michigan, they are reminded of the hour time difference when they interact with the local community. The clock repeatedly reminds them that "home" and "retreat" are different worlds. I feel similarly when I make a summer trek to New Brunswick, Canada. Although we stay less than a week and are fewer than a dozen miles from the U.S. border, we feel more severed from our normal lives by experiencing a change in the clock.

The idea of a second home as a retreat is hardly new. The Romans discovered the allure of second home life two thousand years ago, seeking an escape from the demands and restrictions of society. "There is no need for a toga, the neighbors do not come to call, it is always quiet and peaceful—advantages as great as the healthful situation and limpid air," wrote Pliny the Younger of his villa outside ancient Rome. In 1559, when Giuseppe Falcone visited his Italian country house, he reveled in eating lots of garlic and doing menial chores such as toting firewood without "losing face" with friends. *House Beautiful* reported in 1970 that second-home owners "don't concern themselves so much about sand on the floor or an unmade bed."

The crowds, noise, and dirt of city life, as well, have long inspired urban dwellers to seek the antidote of nature. In 1869, Reverend William Murray wrote *Adventures in the Wilderness; or Camp Life in the Adirondacks,* one of several books that romanticized rustic vacations and closeness with nature at a time of enormous technological change and urbanization. Interest in the Adirondacks led to the creation of the "great camps," extravagant log compounds built by entrepreneur William West Durant. Following Durant's style, summer folk connected with nature by crafting birchbark butter plates, twig furniture, and gun racks cobbled from deer hooves. It's easy to forget, as well, that Thoreau's cottage at Walden Pond was actually a second home, not many miles from his primary abode. From ancient Rome to modern times, the attractions of landscape have been a prime inspiration for acquiring what is, after all, often called a "country home."

Still, the role that second homes play in our lives today is changing. (For one, they are no longer necessarily country houses—ten percent of second homes are in the city.) With our primary homes increasingly becoming public, frenzied

places of busyness—headquarters or base camps of living—
people are searching with a new urgency for a retreat. With
the lines between work and home, public and private,
strangers and intimates blurring, they are rediscovering the
boundary of landscape as a shelter from the world. As a
result, second homes are becoming year-round, alternative
homes—a domestic alter ego. Perhaps never before have so
many people outside the aristocracy invested so much in
dividing their lives between two houses. In doing so, they
may be unconsciously echoing a lost inspiration for
acquiring a second home.

For centuries, the inspiration behind country homes
alternated between a drive for spiritual value and
enjoyment of more bodily pleasures, according to author
James Ackerman. Ancient Romans looked to their country
homes as places to improve mind and body, and Petrarch
described fourteenth-century villa life as ideally devoted to
intense study and the domination of the unruly human
spirit. But three hundred years later, simple pleasures
dominated. Agostino Gallo described a sixteenth-century
vacation house "fishing party" in which nobles watched
peasants drain a small pond, then slip comically in the mud
as they tried to catch fish barehanded. By the eighteenth
century, the country home as pleasure house had won out,
eclipsing any drive for self-improvement or moral value in
these homes away from home.

Yet many people today are again looking for more than
fun when they pursue a second home. People such as Rick
Boynton and Criss Henderson are searching to create in
their second home the feeling of sanctuary they can't find in
their first home. They are taking the traditional domestic
function of retreat and giving it an entirely separate setting.
In doing so, they are creating a more flexible definition of
home, one which melds a deep-felt need for sanctuary with
an embracing of mobility. They are pioneers in our twenty-
first century search for home.

*There is, in particular, a potential conflict
between the ideas of home as an activity
center and as a refuge, and resolving this will
require careful planning.*

William Mitchell, *e-topia*

What happens when people bring full-time work into the wild? Boynton and Henderson have imported the tools of work into their second home, yet are trying to preserve the sanctuary of that space. Others are attracted by the idea of bringing full-time work to remote, perhaps exotic areas, creating in effect what I call the "connected refuge." This seemingly paradoxical idea has tantalized people since the dawn of the computer age. In 1968, urbanist Melvin Webber sketched a romantic vision of this idea. "For the first time in history," he wrote, "it might be possible to locate on a mountain top and maintain intimate, real-time and realistic contact with business or other associates."

As if realizing this dream, a recent ad shows a woman in top-of-the-line mountaineering gear, seated upon an Everest-like peak, pecking at her laptop. The advertiser aims to show off the technology, but the scene is seductive because this woman seems to be having her cake and eating it too. She's reveling in nature, untethered to social demands. Yet with a click and tap, she can apparently reenter society whenever she desires. In his book *e-topia*, William Mitchell accurately predicted a surge of people looking to move to those mountaintops to live and work. "We can expect then, that localities capable of one-upping others through their pleasant climates, spectacular scenery, and attractive recreational opportunities will attract not only holidaymakers but also a new class of permanent residents," he writes.

How can this succeed? Doesn't the full integration of work and home on the "mountaintop" create the kind of chaotic jumble of life that we suffer at home so often these days? Landscapes, time zones, and travel are tools— perhaps crutches—we can use in order to draw boundaries around a place of sanctuary. But to realize the getaway that a second home promises, we have to be willing to use and respect those tools. In order to build a truly "connected refuge," we may also have to turn once again to the traditions of the Industrial Age, which value the separation of work and home.

Jim Hanlon and his wife Maddy have done just that in dividing their time between homes on sparkling blue bays in Florida and Rhode Island. A consultant who has lived around the world, Jim Hanlon telecommutes full-time from both of their homes. Yet he's so contented with this lifestyle that he doesn't take vacations. The Hanlons have redefined home in their own way, and, in doing so, built a home life that bridges the twentieth and twenty-first centuries.

One chilly fall afternoon, I visited their house on Goat Island, a tiny spot of land connected by a causeway to the sailing mecca of Newport. They were just days away from their annual trek to their Florida home, and Hanlon kept going outside to check on the workmen fixing their back deck. But he ignored the persistent ringing of his work telephone in a basement office. Sipping a glass of minty iced tea, he told the story of how he and Maddy wound up dividing their time between two "alternate homes."

Years ago, the couple bought a Florida condo as an investment, but came to enjoy the area so much that they stopped renting it in order to spend more time there themselves. They were living in Connecticut, and were feeling burdened by the upkeep of the house and the long New England winters. "The house was 5,500 square feet, and I don't think we'd been in the living room in two years," says Hanlon, a trim man who is as solemn as his wife is cheery. With technology making his work portable, and their children grown, they sold the Connecticut house and bought the Newport condominium—embarking on a life divided between two smaller homes. "When the dog and the cat died, that was it! That's it, man, we're now free," said Hanlon.

"Home" and "place" need not be rigidly wed.

Hanlon is quick to say, however, that they do not live in two *vacation* homes. When he's not traveling, Hanlon begins work in Rhode Island or Florida by 7:30 in the morning. He works a full day, then pops out of his home office and yells jokingly, "Maddy, I'm home!" before having an evening cocktail. Maddy ships her computer and household files from Rhode Island to Florida in October and back again each May. When they want peace or fun, they need only step outside—using the landscape, as other second homeowners do—as a powerful reminder of the need to retreat from the busyness of the day. Up north, his house is not big or showy, and sits in a line of similar townhouse condos. But the surroundings, a busy harbor speckled with snow-white boats, is stunning. In Florida, they can see the sun setting over the Gulf of Mexico from their condo. "I don't feel the need to take vacation trips, because I can, if it's warm, sit on the beach every weekend," said Hanlon. "You're in a resort area all the time." In essence, neither house is a getaway from the other house, or from another life. The couple carry their entire selves, not just their work self or relaxation self, from one place to another in an organized ritual.

This style of life succeeds because the Hanlons have married Industrial Age work habits with a flexible vision of home. Although his job is predicated on using technology to work anywhere, Hanlon has learned how to keep his work contained within his work day. "When the office is closed, it's closed," he says. At the same time, they are truly comfortable with the mobility of home, partly because they lived abroad for so many years. In their numerous foreign postings, they learned that "home" and "place" need not be rigidly wed. Just as nomads can have an iron-strong sense of family and home despite constant moves through the landscape, the Hanlons settled in each new city through the comfort of their possessions and their closeness as a family. "By the time you got in and got the furniture put down and hung up some pictures and made the beds, the kids felt at home," recalls Jim.

Surely, a sense of place is an important ingredient in the recipe for home. That's one reason why our memories of home are often built on sensory experiences, from the smell of our father's pillow to the comforting creak of a long-ago staircase. I was a bit glad when, during our stays in borrowed apartments, my children would sniffle into their beds at night, missing their own home. In one particularly palatial space, my seven-year-old moaned, "I don't like this drafty old place! I want to go home." The ability to revere place—whether a landscape or a particular house—makes us better able to make a retreat. Yet the experience of Jim and Maddy Hanlon shows us that the rituals, intimacy, and comforts of home are not dependent *only* on a particular four walls or one view. Their new life, divided between two homes, underscores the idea that mobility and home can coexist.

Home Is Where You Are.

Ford announcement for Windstar
Solutions van

If mobility and home can coexist, does this mean we can make homes anywhere—"in the tent, the lodging house, the vestibuled car, the ocean steamer," in Anna McClure Sholl's words? We seem to be trying. Along with importing home into the workplace, a trend that raises the specter of a kind of job-based homelessness, Americans are searching for home in places from automobiles to hotels. This trend offers the possibility of a mobility far beyond that of owning two homes, and begs important questions. If work has been freed from the confines of the office, can we make home portable? Do we want to?

"Bringing the convenience of home to the vehicle." That's the idea, Ford says, behind the Windstar Solutions minivan, a concept vehicle designed in cooperation with appliance maker Maytag. The Windstar looks like a run-of-the-mill minivan on the outside, but its interior takes an unusual turn. The vehicle features a microwave and washer-dryer, two refrigerator drawers, seat-back tray tables, hot-and-cold cup holders, wet-or-dry vacuum, a computer connection to home appliances, and a trash compactor. A one-of-a-kind, the van isn't intended for immediate production. Rather, the companies wanted to gauge consumer reaction to the idea of extending "home" to the car. Ford and Maytag bypassed auto shows to unveil the Windstar Solutions at a kitchen and bath trade show, then shipped the van to state fairs, and even a women's conference. Many people loved it and others grumbled. Marjorie Ryan, a mother viewing the van at the Minnesota State Fair, remarked that the idea that we need appliances everywhere we go is a "sad commentary on the pace of our lives today."

With or without appliances, Americans spend an enormous amount of time in their cars, a trend Ford researchers have been noting in their focus groups. "It wasn't uncommon for people to say they'd eat two meals a day in their vehicles," says Linda Lee, director of women's marketing at Ford. "That isn't counting the road warrior, people who literally use their cars for work. I'm talking about ordinary people like you and me who have other kinds of jobs."

The car-as-kitchen is just one of the ways in which we're treating the automobile as a portable home. Nowadays, cars are moving home offices, with cell phone calls and voice-activated e-mail juggled with driving. A general contractor, tired of the mess he made in his car while working, created the $280 Executive Auto Desk, which fits on the passenger seat and features room for a laptop and storage for office supplies. American vehicles are also the new family room, featuring TV/video equipment with remote controls, voice recorders, satellite navigation systems, and more. "Something domestic, as in cozy, has crept into car DNA," writes *The New York Times*. "It all started with cup holders, of course. But now minivans and other vehicles are being invaded by a flood of appliances and living room fixtures, from dual climate controls to computer game systems. . . ." Indeed, the way people use their cars, just as the way they experience their second homes, tells us a great deal about our changing attitudes toward home.

"Mr. Demas, is there an emergency in your vehicle? Mr. Demas? Mr. Demas, if you don't answer, I will have to send out the police."

I'm watching a plump woman with a telephone headset speak from her desk in suburban Detroit directly into Mr. Demas' car as he drives through Sacramento, California. As an "adviser" with General Motors' wireless OnStar system, her job is to determine if Mr. Demas has had an accident, needs help or, more likely, pushed the OnStar emergency button in his car by mistake. She can notify emergency services if his airbag is inflated, open his car if he's locked out, direct him street by street through Sacramento if he's lost, and more. OnStar and its competitors in the fast-growing automotive telematics field are helping to redefine the role of the car in our lives.

Along with becoming a moving extension of our homes, the car is evolving into a kind of mechanized domestic servant. As well as eating, working, and playing in our cars, we expect to accomplish chores or errands *in* our cars, not just in places we reach *by* car. A significant portion of calls to OnStar, for example, involve convenience or concierge services. That means that, for free or for a monthly fee depending on the model, OnStar advisers or a concierge service will locate ATMs, gas stations, or hard-to-get restaurant reservations for customers. At the call center I visited, advisers get a rush of phone calls most evenings around midnight from travelers who don't know where they're staying that night. Such timing certainly indicates a willingness to put your personal affairs in OnStar's hands. Before OnStar drew the line, early subscribers asked the concierge service to make hair and dentist appointments, give wake-up calls, and do personal shopping. "We had people who would call up and say, 'I'm going to such-and-such a bar, could you please call ahead and have two dry, vodka martinis waiting for me? Joe the bartender knows me,'" said Mike Peterson, an OnStar executive.

The yearning for home outside of home is so strong that the trend is inspiring new types of vacation accommodations that are a cross between second homes and hotel rooms, such as the "fractional ownership" clubs developed by upscale hotel chains including Ritz Carlton. Unlike time-share owners who return to the same unit repeatedly, club members can spend about a month annually at condos or hotels nationwide. Such clubs infuse the time-share concept with greater mobility. Hotel suites and condo rentals are also in demand.

*We shouldn't mistake cars or hotels as
substitutes for home.*

Families are drawn to such spaces because they're often
seeking to create on vacation the sanctuary they no longer
find at home. Travelers of all sorts are spending more time
than ever in their hotel rooms, hence they want comforts
beyond a television and mini-bar. While hotel children's
programs are well-used, the number of hours children
spend in the programs is dropping. "You think, as a parent,
what's going to create a quality time experience? Space and
conveniences and a setting of home," says Nancy Schretter,
president of the Family Travel Network, a consulting and
market research firm. "You'd just love to have this kind of
time 365 days a year in a perfect world, but it's just not
possible anymore."

The drive to find "home" outside our primary abode
shows me how hungry we are for the comforts of home.
And that is not so bad. In a mobile society, at a time when
we can be connected and informed and tapped day and
night, we may need to start feeling more at home in a world
that's not always local and comprehensible. Still, we can't
make a home anywhere. If we're nuking our supper in the
minivan because we never find the time to sit down and eat
together, we're losing our ability to make a home. If we look
to our five-day vacation in a rented condo to make up for all
the missed conversation and time together of the year, we're
losing our ability to make a home. We should feel at home
in the world, and learn to carry with us the sanctuary we
need to survive as human beings. But we shouldn't mistake
cars or hotels as substitutes for home.

In his book *The Domestication of the Human Species,*
anthropologist Peter Wilson explains his view that
hunter/gatherer societies navigate the world primarily
through the prism of "focus," while domesticated societies
emphasize boundaries. His theory deserves consideration
as a way of understanding the present and perhaps our
future. Industrialization marked the zenith of a society of
boundary making, while computers propel us into a world

we navigate through focus. Now, we are struggling between these two worlds.

In many nomadic hunter/gatherer societies, Wilson wrote, people identify with ever-changing points in a landscape. Boundaries are hazy and relationships are flexible and fluid, with a great deal of individual self-sufficiency expected. Relationships are often personal, not formal or rule-governed. By the age of five or six, for example, a child from the Pandaram people in India ceases to have close emotional ties to his parents. "Without boundaries and without the *concept* of the permanent boundary, people are not conceptually locked into their relationships or surroundings," writes Wilson.

In contrast, the creation of permanent settlements, starting about 15,000 years ago, radically changed people's world-view. With the institution of architecture, "time becomes repetition and recursiveness—the same things happen at different times in the same place—birth, death, growth, decay, ripeness, seasons, comings and goings," according to Wilson. In particular, the house becomes a center for and prism of the universe, an anchor for mankind. In ancient Greece, a man who did not own a house could not take part "in the affairs of the world because he had no location in it which was properly his own," Hannah Arendt writes.

Our society looks more and more like a system based on "focus," not boundaries. Our relationships at work, home, and in the community are increasingly fluid, in large part due to the influence of technology. Think of the demise of the traditional family, and the rise in free agent careers and mobility in work. In the Internet Age, you can work with, love, learn about, and relate to people without even knowing where they live. No matter where you are, your day is likely to be increasingly shaped by choices in what you focus on—the TV, pager, e-mail, cell phone, the road ahead, your cubicle-mate. Yet unlike humans 20,000 years ago, we also must deal with multiple landscapes and groups of people—all at the same time.

Our search for homes outside our home shows me that we are not entirely comfortable in a boundary-less society defined by "focus." Maybe someday we will be, and then perhaps we will have no need of home as a sanctuary. But for now, we still need to preserve places where cyclical time and stability can be found, where we can redraw boundaries around our closest relations and ourselves. Home allows us to "create an area of peace, calm and security . . . where we can leave the world and listen to our own rhythm," writes Olivier Marc. "For once we have crossed the threshold and shut the door behind us, we can be at one with ourselves."

In this transitional age, however, home needn't be one rigidly defined place. Boundaries that cannot be crossed create prisons. "Incessant occupation is not essential to a home," pleaded Charlotte Perkins Gilman in 1903 as she tried to liberate women from the Cult of Domesticity that so often enslaved them. We can find home in a second home as domestic alter ego or a connected refuge. We can make home a more flexible concept in an age that is halfway between "boundaries" and "focus." We can be both mobile and anchored in a rapidly changing world. But we can't mistake any place for a home. We should be at home in the world, while keeping a home for ourselves.

Diary: Campobello

We are visiting St. Andrew's, a little town in Canada near Franklin Delano Roosevelt's childhood summer cottage. One day, we take a car ride, then two ferry trips in a pea soup fog to get to his house on the island of Campobello. By the time we arrive, the morning mists have cleared, and we can see the cool-blue ocean stretching beyond the red-shingled Roosevelt cottage set on a grassy hill.

The house, where FDR spent summers from infancy to the time he contracted polio in his early 20s, is a restful place. Dark wood and floral wallpaper line plain rooms. Nubby white bedspreads lie on family beds. The house seems simple and summer-like. Nothing is grand. I find myself thinking of scrapbooks and card games—summer rituals that take time.

During our own weeklong vacation, we try to strike a balance between activity and rest. We take long walks, sleep in, and make time to lick ice cream cones and write postcards (although no letters). Still, there are many moments when I catch myself hurrying the children, just as we do at home—"C'mon! Time for a swim! Get dressed for dinner!" When we arrive on Campobello Island, we stop for lunch at a picturesque fish restaurant, then grow tense when the service is slow and our quick bite drags on for more than an hour. I'm not sure whether we are squeezing all the best out of each day, or trying—as so often happens at home—to do too much.

FDR's father was wealthy and lived at a time when the aristocracy often had nothing but time for pursuits we now see as leisure: art, scholarly reading, intellectual conversation, gardening. I wouldn't want such a life, no matter how accomplished. Nevertheless, the thought of having a whole summer stretch before me seems heavenly. Too many Americans these days work so hard they don't notice the changes in season, the shift of the constellations, the rhythm of the landscape. They don't have time to enjoy the possessions their earnings buy. When we went to Campobello Island, I felt jealous that the Roosevelts' summer truly lasted all summer, unbroken by work.

This summer, we also stopped in Rhode Island, and found ourselves thinking about buying a cottage. I don't think this was ever more than an impulse, but we enjoyed mulling over this possibility and its ramifications for our home life. We've been visiting a friend in Rhode Island for the past few years, and once rented a house for two weeks in an area so quiet that the nearest supermarket is twenty miles away. The village has a general store, diner, pizzeria, vegetable stand, and fish market. Otherwise, all is farmland, salty river, and the Atlantic Ocean.

Stopping on the way back from Canada, we tempted ourselves by calling a realtor and looking at a few small houses. One tiny sliver of land overlooking a salt marsh beckoned. I could envision myself on the deck of this house, reading a book (that had nothing to do with work), as the kids played on the lawn. We drove back and forth, stopping three times to swat mosquitoes and wet our feet in every corner of the marshy land. We visualized which pieces of furniture we would transfer from our full-to-the-gills New York apartment.

Perhaps we seek a second house because we've destroyed the sanctuary of our own home—with work, busy schedules, technology. Integrating work into home especially is flexible but ceaseless. At home, there's a monkey on my shoulder, night and day. Foregoing work for twenty-four hours is rare. Trying in another way to justify the idea of a Rhode Island house, my husband began contemplating how I could go there and write without interruption. But if I did that, I'd be re-creating the conundrum of my home all over again: where do I put my laptop, and how much work is enough? How do we learn to slow down?

S I X

Ett Hem (A Home):
An Ever-Evolving Canvas for
Human Relations

We will not go back to basics. We will go forward to basics.

Swedish physicist Bodil Jönsson

I am stepping into a painting. Warm sunshine splashes on a weathered pine floor, on white-painted chairs with blue-checked cushions, on geraniums lining a windowsill. Outside, a chilly river rushes by a snowy landscape. Within, the room is airy and embracing—and familiar. I am at home, on a wintry afternoon in the forested heart of Sweden, in a 150-year-old farmhouse where I've never been before.

This is Lilla Hyttnäs, the house of Carl Larsson, a nineteenth-century painter whose crisp watercolors of domestic life are known to every Swede. His stately murals hang in the Royal Opera House and National Museum in Stockholm, but he's most famous for his intimate glimpses of life in this house—summer picnics under a birch tree, little girls at play in striped pinafores, a dog dozing in a pool of sunlight in the living room. One painting depicts a children's bedroom in the early morning: beds are unmade, wooden blocks scatter across the floor, a baby plays with a cup as a small girl dressed in nothing but loose black stockings smiles at the viewer, her white nightgown clutched in hand.

There is no American equivalent of Lilla Hyttnäs, no single house in the United States that represents the essence of home for us. The log cabin is a symbol, rooted in the past. Monticello, the Virginia plantation lovingly designed by Thomas Jefferson, is famous yet a statesman's creation, its place in our national psyche colored by its roots in slavery.

The Larsson house, in contrast, is an icon of home in Sweden. Larsson and his wife Karin, also an artist, crafted the house in a spartan but warm style that foreshadowed modern Swedish design. Even a hip, young Stockholmer today would acknowledge its visual power, and perhaps make the trek to the tiny village of Sundborn to see the house. Each summer, Lilla Hyttnäs, or "little copper island," draws 60,000 visitors—eighty percent of whom are Swedes. "They recognize the house. They've seen it in paintings," says Lasse Larsson-Hytte, a gruff Carl Larsson grandson who has opened the house for my visit. "This is the heart of Sweden for them."

In Sweden, the idea of home itself is venerated.

Visiting Sweden in the depths of winter, I begin to understand the almost primeval lure of home in this country. As I ride north from Stockholm one morning on the train, streetlights and car headlights shine on trees eerily cloaked in silvery ice—at 10 a.m. By mid-afternoon, pink streaks of a setting sun are brushed across the sky and the cold is numbing. As if to beat back the encroaching darkness each afternoon, candles are lit almost everywhere, even in office buildings. I realize that the importance of Lilla Hyttnäs to Swedes lies not just in its vision, at once traditional and modern, of how a home should look. The fascination goes beyond gingham or painted cupboards, for it is understood by those who abhor them. In Sweden, the idea of home itself is venerated—even at the dawn of the Internet Era. Perhaps this old farmhouse can help point me to the future of home in a mobile and technological age.

Like Lilla Hyttnäs, this is a nation with roots firmly in the countryside. Dirt-poor Sweden didn't industrialize until the late 1800s, a century after Britain. From this hardscrabble past, the Social Democrats arose in the 1920s to map out a vision of a collective society called the "people's home." The legacy of their half century of government has led to parental leaves now totaling 450 days, mostly at eighty percent pay, and a revered tradition of five weeks annual vacation. Private life has been fiercely protected in Sweden. And yet this country, more than any other, is hurtling into the computer era, with all the sweeping changes to home and work life that technology brings. More than half of all Sweden's 8.9 million people use the Internet, and more than seventy percent have mobile phones. How is a nation rooted in a slower, rural era coping with its embrace of gadgets that erode the boundaries of time and space? How will the idea of home evolve in the Information Age? Many Swedes are asking such questions.

Before I arrived, a two-page spread in a new Swedish magazine devoted to the wireless industry caught my eye. A watercolor in Carl Larsson style shows a family in the dining room at Lilla Hyttnäs, where the Larssons and their seven children shared a long wooden table. The picture's warm colors, striped pinafores, geraniums on the windowsill are all modeled after a 1901 Larsson painting. But while one child in the illustration is making a pie, another is using a tiny laptop, and a boy wears a cell phone on his belt. In a corner, a smart refrigerator has signaled that the family needs milk. "Science fiction films must have indoctrinated us to believe that computerized creatures are most comfortable among hard, polished plastic. But humans are not changed so easily," writes the illustrator, Kerstin Kåll. "Even IT consultants can like hand-woven rag rugs. Even programmers can water the geraniums." I think of this mélange of old and new as I walk through the Larsson house, now used by the artist's descendents for family get-togethers or holiday visits.

A stout septuagenarian with ice-blue eyes, Lasse Larsson-Hytte is an engineer who traveled the world building enormous mining machines. He isn't gregarious, sometimes answering my questions with a brief "Op" or "Har." But he obviously loves this house and its story. Although his grandparents died a few years before he was born, he lived here for four years as a boy, and he returns frequently. In his grandmother's weaving workshop, he bends down before an open fireplace and fiddles with the top of a child's miniature wrought-iron stove. "This was Karin's stove when she was a little girl," says Larsson-Hytte. "In the summer, we take it outside and make wonderful pancakes." I look. He holds a small, heart-shaped pancake mold.

A few steps away, he lifts a sheet under the stairs, and his eyes twinkle. Underneath is a big, black TV, brought out for the times when the Larsson family stays here once more.

Jörgen Lerjestad, a slightly built man with an easygoing manner, is nursing a cup of coffee one morning while sitting in a brightly colored conference room atop one of Stockholm's few skyscrapers. This twenty-four-story building and surrounding complex, built in 1962, were named after Axel Wenner-Gren, a Swedish scientist who founded appliance maker Electrolux and who fervently believed that technology could solve human ills. In this case, however, Wenner-Gren Center is home to an IT company founded to put human needs ahead of technology's demands.

Lerjestad's story begins in the early 1990s on the day when, in his words, he felt his mortality for the first time. He'd been working for years in Sweden's breakneck IT culture, while raising a family. One day, however, he went to do a spellcheck on his PC and found that he had to enlarge the text nearly 400 percent before he could focus on the words. For the first time, he sensed his limitations. "I realized this couldn't go on," he recalls. "You can work twenty-four hours a day and you can skip seeing your children for weeks and you can think that's all right, but at the end of the day you don't feel well and you're not as efficient as you think you are."

Bear in mind that Lerjestad came to this conclusion while Sweden was catching the world's attention as a center for high-tech innovation. Beginning in the 1970s, Sweden became a world leader in use of mobile phones and workplace computers. By 2000, media and market researchers had dubbed Stockholm "Europe's Internet capital," within the "most wired and wireless nation." Behemoths such as Microsoft and Intel chose to base important wireless research operations in Sweden, center of the Scandinavian "Wireless Valley." The excitement in the 1990s was palpable and the riches were immense, just as in the United States. It's easy now, after stock market nose-dives and layoffs, to imagine questioning the era's go-get-'em work ethic. Yet in those early days, that's just what Lerjestad did. In 1998, he founded Peak Six, a web design and IT consultancy that gives its employees a six-hour workday while paying them for eight hours.

Even in a country without a tradition of workaholism, it did not prove easy to fiddle with the Industrial Age standards of work. Lerjestad at first felt guilty leaving with what seemed like half the workday still before him, until he took up pursuits such as chess and running. Another employee was embarrassed to notice that in mid-afternoon, he shared the streets with only retirees and mothers with small children. "In the first month, I didn't work one single day that was six hours," recalls art director Brian Richards, a tall, trim Brit who is a passionate mountain biker. "But then I found that by 3:30 the office was empty apart from me. Everyone else had managed to go home. I kind of realized, 'just try it.'"

The concept seems to contradict traditional rules of profitability. "If you work six hours instead of eight, you have two hours less that you can produce," says Lerjestad in sometimes choppy English. "We meet skepticisms." But Lerjestad believes that most people aren't effective the entire workday, and become more productive if private chores are taken care of after work. In time, Lerjestad has found that his employees make fewer mistakes because they are more focused. Clients, of course, don't mind being billed for fewer hours.

The six-hour day is just one way of showing things can be done in a different manner.

Tim Finucane

Unusual even by Sweden's generous standards, the Peak Six philosophy is gaining attention. Part-time work is much more readily available in Sweden than in the United

States (about forty percent of Swedish women work part-time), but such schedules still carry pay cuts. Lerjestad's ideas have been so well-received that he now spends most of his time teaching other companies how to do similar experiments. His staff numbers twenty, although at any one time, not all work on the six-hour schedule. If employees need to stay until midnight to finish a project, they do, although they then might leave early the next day. "You have to remember this is an experiment," chimes in an employee, Tim Finucane. "The six-hour day is not like a holy principle that should never be broken. It's just one way of showing things can be done in a different manner."

Certainly, this is one way of showing that private life still matters at a time when the pace of life is accelerating. During my two-week visit, one television program aired and two conferences took place in greater Stockholm on stress and burnout—problems that are new on such a scale in modern Sweden. For years, strong unions and a pro-labor government kept overtime in check, while high taxes and cradle-to-grave welfare benefits discouraged American-style workaholism. But nowadays, even outside IT culture, working hours are climbing steadily. In 1997, nearly sixty percent of Swedes felt they had too much to do at work, up from about fifty percent in 1989 and about par with current American feelings of overwork. And as in the United States, such pressures cross gender boundaries, since nearly eighty percent of women of working age have jobs. Although they may not have a history of overwork and still take long vacations, Swedes are coping with challenges we know well: the time bind of dual-earner parents and the weariness of the job-stressed.

Many Swedes are cognizant of the role technology is playing in this melting pot of millennial ills. This wired society is increasingly talking about the pros and cons of being "always connected." While the long summer vacation is still observed, its sacredness is waning as people log on at the cottage and answer work calls from their boats. The changes brought by mobile technology provide a talking point for Ingemar Olsson, a Volvo engineer who devoted a sixteen-month sabbatical to founding a government-backed program to improve work-life balance for Swedish men. In his travels,

Olsson soon realized he could get corporate men to open up about their home lives if he raised the subject of mobile phones and laptops. "It's a very good way to discuss what's important for men, their values, their family life, how to bring more time with the families," says Olsson. "Technology changes the family life. . . . It's a double-edged sword."

These trends trouble Lisbeth Gustafsson, head of sales for Posten, the Swedish post office's Internet subsidiary. After working at Digital computers for thirteen years, she started the post office's first portal for e-commerce, and helped design a workplace that reflects the venture's high-tech mission. "We are working with e-commerce solutions, we are working with a new market, we are representing a new way of doing business, and that has to be shadowed in the way we work ourselves," Gustafsson says briskly as she whirls me through Posten's brightly colored offices in suburban Stockholm.

In a hall right next to the front door, she shows me her "office"—a few shelves in a small wooden cabinet. Posten aims to be entirely wireless, so people plant their laptops and cell phones each day at softly curving tables and keep paper to a minimum. Gustafsson, in fact, is so mobile that she does most of her work on a table that's a five-minute walk from her "office." To echo the theme of mobility, Gustafsson gave the workplace a nautical design. Furniture is bright red, white, and blue, after the colors of international signal flags. Workers make private phone calls in lighthouse-shaped phone booths dotting the space. "I personally think this is the best thing that has happened to mankind, that you can work wherever you are!" says Gustafsson. As I trail behind her long stride, I begin to see her as a modern Viking. Her forebears sought land, while she pursues new ways to conquer time and space. Like an explorer, she's both excited and cautious about the unknown.

Although she has two mobile phones, plus a printer, fax, PC, and laptop at home, and telecommutes one day a month, she draws firm boundaries around her private life. Perhaps that's because she had never touched a computer until almost the age of forty. "I decided from the very beginning to take control over the technology, not the other way around," she says. As a result, she keeps her work cell phone off from Friday night to Monday morning, and does not check e-mail on weekends or vacations. Her secretary can call her, but only in an extreme emergency. "The reason we see a lot of burnout today has to do with availability," she says. "I don't think the human body, the human brain are made to be connected twenty-four hours, seven days a week. Not in the long run."

Gustafsson has seen young employees burn out at Posten, and she knows the advances to come will lead to the possibility of even more connectivity. One of her two twenty-something daughters has given up having a cell phone altogether, although Gustafsson says she couldn't imagine doing the same. Like Jörgen Lerjestad, she believes that retaining a private life is crucial, but that it's possible to do so while living with technology. "I think we need those spots where you can be yourself, where no one can reach you basically, so you relax," she muses. "And of course, the spot number one has to be your private home!"

Before I go, she walks me to the door, and leaves me with a final thought. "People are not stressed by hard work, as long as they control their time," says Gustafsson, giving me a firm handshake. "When you lose control of time, that's when the negative stress comes in." During the subway ride back to town, I reflect on all we discussed: private life, technology, mobility. During our hours together, she didn't once take a call from the phone that she kept at her side.

The backlash against the idea of having so much fun at work—we saw that coming years ago.

Johan Ljungman

Across town, Rikard Lindström pushes open a door in the basement of the Internet portal company Spray. Inside are six bunk beds, all neatly made but for one, which has been slept on. Lindström, one of the company's founders, looks surprised. "Oh, they're still used," he says with a shrug, closing the door.

Spray's sprawling offices are in Östermalm, ground zero for many of the capital's 4,200 Internet-related companies. (And this, in a city of about 750,000 people.) The historically posh neighborhood is now ultra-trendy, home to sleek design stores and candlelit café-bars that are jammed with young people each evening. Perhaps the most famous landmark in the area is the black-and-steel Lydmar Hotel, where Sweden's pair of twenty-something royal princesses can be spotted listening to jazz. If Stockholm is, according to one researcher, "the most vibrant hotbed of Internet innovation outside of the United States," then Östermalm is the heart of the hotbed.

And I have come to see Spray's beds. I am interested in how private life is viewed within the IT culture fueling Sweden's race into the computer era. Perhaps the young people who are living the high-tech future don't agree with Lisbeth Gustafsson's fierce devotion to the boundaries of her private life. In the past few years, IT workplaces have become more home-like in Stockholm, just as in the United States. Playspaces, washing machines, sofas, and kitchens abound. Still, I hear stories of a rebellion against these perks by workers tired of living at the office. "Spray has taken out the beds!" several people tell me. "You should check it out." They are wrong. Nevertheless, the beds may be symbolically on their way out.

Lindström, a boyish-faced man with punkish hair, at first won't talk to me, but finally agrees to meet at Spray's offices. He remains skittish, telling me that Spray had beds long ago at an office outside Stockholm. Finally he warms to the conversation and, choosing his words carefully, begins to describe how a respect for private life has become a bigger part of company culture. "We were rebels. We believed anything could be digital," he said, explaining why endless work hours dominated the company's early days in the mid-1990s. After a few years, Lindström and his coworkers learned to prioritize, partly due to having families. Lindström says that nowadays, if he needs to call a colleague during the weekend concerning a project due Monday, he'll wait at least until Sunday evening so he doesn't spoil his colleague's Saturday.

I ask for a tour, and we go to a dimly lit basement, where cavernous rooms are used for parties and meetings. There is a red plush conference room with a white plastic table, a purple bar with a disco-like feel. The "trash room"—where you can "trash" things—sports handprints on the walls and wooden stick figures dangling from the ceiling. Behind a wall decorated with a throbbing red neon light is an auditorium with bucket-chairs. "The impression is like going into a Star Trek room," mutters Lindström. Last, he offers a quick peek at the bedroom, the only room without a futuristic design. He is practically sprinting through this last part of our interview. He's mentioned that he has another appointment, but he reminds me of a man hurrying by his childhood bedroom, embarrassed to look at his outgrown past.

Another morning, I meet three young men in black for breakfast in the Lydmar Hotel, where hip music throbs and lattés flow as a gray dawn spreads across Stockholm. Working around the corner from Spray, they are some of the main research consultants for E2, a project by Ericsson and Electrolux to design the future home. But when I mention Spray and the trend toward more homelike offices, they momentarily leave behind observations on the future. With words tumbling, they heatedly tell me what they think about beds at work or washers in the office: workers in the IT world want their private lives back.

A few years ago, the young men's company began serving breakfast to the staff, an innovation that drew media headlines. I immediately thought about Agency.com's pancake breakfast in New York, an experiment to build community and get employees to work earlier. The Swedish firm was also trying to get employees into work—but with the hope that they would go home at a reasonable hour. "We realized that to give that much input and creativity and time and energy, you need input from other areas than your work and colleagues," says Johan Ljungman, head of marketing for Kabel New Media.

He and his coworkers see a growing desire to separate work and home. "There was a tendency a couple of years ago to put in laundry at offices, put in a day care," he says. "Of course, the first reaction is, 'Great, then I'll have time to do my laundry.' But a lot of people began to say, 'That's the only time nowadays I'm by myself, and can think for two hours. And I don't want to bring my laundry in, because they know I will stay longer to do it! I want to separate my private life.'" His company considered installing a laundry at work, but decided that this would keep people at the office too long.

Despite these efforts, burnout still occurs. "I'm thinking of a young kid at our company, he was there every night, all night, every morning. We thought he had fun, we thought he liked it, because he played games and knew everybody. But he got totally burned out. He became a lousy employee because he couldn't do anything anymore." One summer, Ljungman became the first person in his company to take a three-month sabbatical, inspiring others to follow suit.

> *Private life doesn't always come first in Sweden, but it's still respected.*

Peak Six. Postnet. Spray. In varying ways, these companies are wrestling with ways to preserve the rapidly disappearing boundaries between home and work. Jörgen Lerjestad gives his workers the time to take care of chores outside work, so they work productively but still have other lives. Lisbeth Gustafsson is a technophile who openly draws firm boundaries around her home. Rikard Lindström is trying to live a full life, not at the beck and call of work. I began to see—in the attention given Peak Six, in the fascination with Spray's beds—a groundswell of support for their efforts. Private life doesn't always come first in Sweden, but it's still respected in the computer age.

When I mentioned reading an article about Americans removing kitchens from their homes, many Swedes were dumbstruck. Even the young researchers at the Lydmar Hotel were incredulous. "People might microwave food here, but they would still sit together at the dinner table," said Staffan Bane, creative director for Kabel. Households, including growing numbers of stepfamilies or cohabiting couples, try hard to eat together. "The kitchen table is a symbol for informality, tradition, rationality, simplicity," writes architect Ulla Westerberg of the Royal Institute of Technology, in a study of eight hundred households' attitudes toward home. Partly due to the climate and the isolation of peasant farms, Sweden never developed a tradition of gathering in cafés or pubs, as other Europeans did. Guests are still usually entertained at home, rather than in restaurants.

Homemade foods, too, predominate. "Especially families with children have very high ambitions when it comes to food and meals," observed Westerberg. "Food ought to be home-made and meals ought to be prepared and eaten together." That goal isn't always reached, but the effort is there. Most Swedes still expect to eat a hot lunch at noon. A cold sandwich won't do. Women supervise weekday cooking, but men often take over on weekends. Before my trip, I asked a Ph.D. candidate who had helped me what I could bring him from the United States, and he requested chocolate chips, having fallen in love with tollhouse cookies during a trip to California. As I presented him with a bag of morsels at a dinner at his home, he gleefully turned to his wife and said, "I'll be baking this weekend, dear!" I couldn't imagine any American male reacting that way, especially in front of a new acquaintance.

Kabel's consumer interviews and focus groups on home laid the ground for the design of E2's pilot development, a refrigerator that allows online access, video-messaging, TV, radio, and food shopping capabilities through a touch screen on the door. During exploratory research, E2 found that Swedish women resisted the idea of putting more technology into their homes, fearing that using the fridge as a communications tool would isolate family members from each other. "It's already gone too far," they told researchers. They felt technology was antisocial. But gradually, they warmed to Screenfridge, in particular to the idea of getting video messages from their children—a sort of twenty-first century note on the counter. Men had a less emotional first reaction, saying they expected Screenfridge to have positive and negative implications for home life, just as all technology does.

Whatever their views on future appliances, the people interviewed—young, old, single, or parents—had strong feelings toward the idea of home, researcher Leif Öhlund said. Home meant "relaxation, security, coziness, a place where I can be myself, where I can get away, feel safe," said Öhlund, adding that the kitchen anchored this idea. To many Swedes, home is still a haven from a fast-paced world, a place where you control the pace of life. A place where you can say no to the cell phone, yes to your daughter's videotaped love note, yes to the satisfying lull of washday. . . . Yes to the future, but not always yes.

The home became a member of the household—a living organism reflecting the constant changes of a growing family.

Michelle Facos writing of Lilla Hyttnäs

A jack-of-all-trades. That is one historian's description of Swedish peasant life before industrialization. Isolated geographically and faced with poor natural resources and land, many Swedes not only grew crops, but raised livestock, fished, hunted, and made crafts to survive. "This complex local economy provided a certain flexibility of lifestyle in Sweden that was not found in many other parts of Europe and it sometimes generated a geographic mobility not found elsewhere," writes historian David Popenoe. In some regions, Swedish peasants moved to various homes at different seasons of the year, taking advantage of the spot with the most abundant resources. Perhaps that's one reason why Swedish summer houses remain so prevalent, even for those of lesser means. About one in twelve Swedes today owns a summer cottage.

Traveling across Sweden in the mid-nineteenth century, Robert Colton peeked into several summer cottages near the capital. "A bed doing duty for a sofa during the day; half a dozen chairs; a table fastened to the tree in front of the cottage; a brass pan or two—serve for a country dwelling's outfit in Sweden—all of which is speedily removed across the lake to the house at Stockholm (in autumn)." He describes a bountiful dinner of herring, sausage, cheese, and other dishes at one of these country huts, where the floor is strewn with juniper and flowers, and the fireplace

and walls are decorated with oak leaves and lilac blossoms.
After supper, guests sat on cushions on the lawn or went
boating.

Carl and Karin Larsson used their cottage in Sundborn
as a summer house for thirteen years. Even after making it
their main home, they often moved the entire household to
Falun, the nearest market center, during the winter so their
children could attend school. The house, too, was always
evolving. "Lilla Hyttnäs underwent constant expansion and
transformation, in both structure and décor," writes art
historian Michelle Facos. Over the years, Larsson painted
family portraits onto the doors and cut a window in his
bedroom wall so he could look down on the work in his
studio each morning with a fresh eye. The exterior of the
house is a pastiche of styles and colors, reflecting many
additions.

Again and again, the Larssons broke rank with tradition
in their décor and use of the house. While the upper classes
of the day devoted different rooms to varying furniture
styles, the Larssons mixed antiques and peasant furniture in
the same room, and did so in an era when peasant crafts
were out of favor. Their use of simple furnishings and
bright greens, reds, and yellows drew from indigenous
culture, and contrasted with the contemporary taste for
dark rooms and overstuffed furniture. Most Swedish homes
of the day stressed sharp hierarchies between private areas
and formal public rooms. Until nearly the turn of the
century, "children usually slept with servants in a small
dark room furnished with 'leftovers,'" writes ethnologist
Orvar Löfgren. But the Larsson house was a seamless whole
in look and feel, where children were welcome from studio
to dining table. "They belonged to the family—the children.
That was very unusual," said the grandson, Larsson-Hytte,
standing in the library where the family read to each other
in the evenings. "That is one of the reasons the children,
when Carl and Karin died, wanted to keep the house. They
spared it."

Lilla Hyttnäs spoke to Swedes even in Carl Larsson's
time. After his watercolors of the interiors were published
in an 1899 book, *Ett Hem (A Home)*, tourists began coming to
Sundborn to see the house. Certainly, the popularity of *Ett*

Hem coincided with the Victorian-era interest in the idea of home as both a refuge and a showcase. Yet the Larssons' willingness to experiment, to blend old and new also appealed to Swedes and their taste for innovation. Observers from Larsson's day consistently noted that Sweden was marked by a mix of "social conservatism and lively interest in novelty." In 1904, O. G. von Heidenstam noted wooden boxes dotting market squares and docks around Stockholm. For a half-penny, a passerby could fill a tin cup with hot milk tapped from these boxes. At automats around the city, a few pennies would buy a sandwich, soup, or tea. It was not until 1912 that New York City's first automat opened.

But what truly impressed von Heidenstam was Stockholm's telephone tower, "a sort of square Eiffel Tower arrested in its growth," from which hundreds of wires radiated across the capital. "For in Sweden," von Heidenstam explained, "the telephone has become a commonplace, and there is not a shop, a house, or an office in Stockholm without it." In 1904, Stockholm's 300,000 people had 30,000 households or offices with telephones, while New York, with a population of 3.4 million, had 27,000. At that time, Stockholm had the world's highest number of telephones per capita.

No wonder Sweden remains a nation of high-tech innovators. Its pioneering role in the Internet Age has a lineage in the multiple roles played by peasants to survive, in their familiarity with mobility, in a national love affair with novelty. Many Swedes have long been willing to experiment with personal technology because they have been innovators in private life. There is a realization that home cannot be a static idea, as shown by the veneration for Lilla Hyttnäs. The Larsson house is admired both as a work of art and as a changing, living home—a reflection of life itself. His descendents treat the house not as a dusty museum where nothing should be touched, but as their own summer house. Today, Swedes still experiment with, yet preserve, the idea of home.

One night in Stockholm, I walked by the Royal Opera House just as the evening's performance ended. The streets filled with people, and while waiting for the light to change, I saw a vivid exhibit of Sweden, the wired society. A young woman in a long fur coat bicycled through the intersection—while dialing her cell phone. She wasn't talking. She was dialing.

Although some Swedes owned mobile telephones as far back as 1985, they've become a facet of daily life just in the past few years. "If you eliminate the very old and the very young, mobile phone ownership rises to about one hundred percent," says Eric Paulak, an analyst in Stockholm with the Gartner Group. Eighty percent of Swedish fifteen- to twenty-year-olds have cell phones, compared with forty percent of that age group in the United States. At the time of my visit, it was not unheard of for an eight-year-old to have one. Furthermore, "mobiles" represent far more than a telephone, they're multi-purpose life tools. When Brian Richards, the mountain-biking art director, asked fourteen guests at a friend's birthday party about their cell phones, he found that half used them as alarm clocks.

Perhaps because cell phones have spread so quickly and completely through Sweden there has been a distinct evolution in the social dynamics of their use. Sure, I heard mobiles ringing in a pool locker room, in restaurants, on trains and subways, although with a musical jingle, not the mechanical ring-ring of most U.S. phones. Still, in increasing numbers of public places, such as hospitals, some train carriages, and fancy restaurants, cell phones are banned. (It's no longer cool, either, to keep your mobile on a restaurant table during dinner.)

The more complicated evolution involves interactions between boss and employee, parent and child, friend to friend, relationships in which connectivity easily clashes with concern for others. Consider work relations. Most Swedish bosses function less as an authoritarian figure and more as a coach, so managers traditionally have not called workers at home. Nowadays it's less taboo to dial a worker's mobile during off-hours, and, since Swedish offices have more of a collective style, workers feel pressure to keep their phones on. Still, I saw plenty of signs that people were experimenting to preserve private life, for both themselves and others. In two years of owning a cell phone and keeping it on twenty-four hours a day, seven days a week, Brian Richards has had only two work phone calls at home.

Perhaps most revealing were my interviews. During two weeks in Sweden, I talked with thirty-nine people, some more formally than others, but most for hours. I talked to them in their offices, kitchens, on a train, over breakfast, lunch, and dinner. In all those conversations, only two people either answered their cell phone or checked their voice-mail messages during our time together—and both were Americans. In fact, they were the only two Americans I talked with. The others—two Danes, a Brit, and the rest Swedes—paid full attention to me, just as they, I assume, wanted me to do for them.

O n my last day in Sweden, I traveled to the south to talk with a woman who personifies this willingness to experiment with technology yet value home. Bodil Jönsson is a physicist who teaches at a Lund University institute devoted to using technology to help the disabled. She became a household name in Sweden after appearing on a television show where experts answer lay people's questions. But she became a kind of guru in 1999 when she wrote a best-selling book on time. Nearly every person I met in Sweden had read *Ten Thoughts About Time*, which was a Swedish bestseller for fourteen months and has been published in eleven other countries, including the United States. Some said her words changed their life. Just as the veneration for Lilla Hyttnäs shows Sweden's respect for home, so this book's popularity signals a willingness to ask hard questions about twenty-first-century life. Jönsson tells a time-starved world that, in fact, we have plenty of time.

Without time, home is an empty shell.

As I taxied through the medieval city of Lund in a chilly drizzle on my way to Jönsson's hilltop office, I thought about how the subject of time has been woven through my search for home in a new age. Without time, home is an empty shell. We need to find the time to eat together, be together, care for each other in order to have home. In her book, Jönsson talks about the many ways we fool ourselves into thinking we are saving time—stuffing our schedules, for instance, with ever more appointments that leave us unable to concentrate on any one thing well. We spend so much of our lives doing little things that we don't take the time to step back and do any one big thing. Finding home, just like finding time, is slippery. It takes effort and thought.

In person, Jönsson combines a scientist's intensity with a grandmother's warmth. She jumps up often to find a paper or picture to illustrate her point, pours coffee for us but barely takes a sip. She gives the impression of being completely enrapt in our meeting. Her determination to be in the "here and now" for whoever she is with is one reason she disdains the mobile phone.

Although she owns one, she barely uses it. She uses e-mail, and relishes in virtual teaching, saying this asynchronous and semi-anonymous method gives her students great freedom to question her in a way they might never dare in person. But the mobile phone "crosses a special border," Jönsson argues. "When you sit here and you are my guest, what I owe you is that I am present here. I don't answer my phone; my thoughts should be here. I have to be now, not later, not before, but now." In contrast, if we choose to be always connected, we are trying to be "here and now" for everybody. "You have to make up your mind," says Jönsson matter-of-factly. "You have to choose between these two things." Always being available makes short-term needs trump long-term goals.

Jönsson crosses the room and returns with an old black-and-white photo, showing a dozen boys and girls posed before a wooden schoolhouse. Behind them stands a woman with a pinched face and a cotton dress, the teacher. Jönsson is one of the thin, little girls sitting on the grass, staring up into the camera. In her childhood, she tells me, the teacher controlled the knowledge. She knew all they were going to learn, and she could dispense this learning as she wished. Contrast this past image of the teacher (or the minister or mayor or CEO) as the center of the universe with the way computers today connect students (or workers or voters) to the world. Technology has empowered all of us to "raise our own questions, and get our own answers," says Jönsson.

This revolution means we all have the responsibility to "make up our minds"—to try and take control of time and of our home lives. The idea of preserving dinnertime or weekends or home seems overwhelming. It's hard to draw the lines. One reason that Jönsson's book has been so popular, she believes, is that it gives people a language to talk about time. "This is about power, and who is to take the first step," she says. "It can be too hard for individuals to say, 'I don't want to use my Sundays.' You need to have somebody behind you."

I thought of Jörgen Lerjestad, who had recently experimented with shutting off the voice mail on his cell phone to recapture a pocket of silence in his day. I thought of Johan Ljungman, who took the first sabbatical in his new media company. I thought of Karin and Carl Larsson, who didn't kowtow to the domestic dictates of their day, who envisioned home as a constantly evolving canvas for human relations. They and other Swedes do not have any one answer as to how we'll create homes in this century, and perhaps they don't have any answer for us at all. But they are taking the time to ask the right questions: How do we preserve the strength of valued traditions while harnessing the power of the new? How do we nurture human relations as we work more closely with machines? How do we keep home alive in a high-tech age?

Diary: Time, Space, and a Table

I've been thinking about time and space, and realizing that I integrate work and home more often in time—less often in the space of my home.

Nowadays, instead of working from nine until six, I might work a bit, then perhaps take time to do grocery shopping, then work, eat with my family and put my children to bed, then work some more. By the end of the day, I'm sometimes making a phone call about the school party, then finishing up reading a research article, then talking to my husband before we crawl to bed, exhausted.

This is the kind of integration of public and private life that will mark the future.

Still, I've been trying unconsciously to make an effort to separate the spaces of my home. I have taken over one corner of our bedroom as my office, spreading my work out on the long dining room table my father built. Although I bring reading work and sometimes my laptop into the kitchen, dining room, or living room, I try not to keep work books or papers in these other rooms. I didn't realize how crucial that was to preserving a sense of home until one day when my husband found a stack of my files in the living room. Uncharacteristically, he snapped, "You've taken over enough of the house! Now I'm losing my whole home to this book."

My husband has uncomplainingly watched me sequester myself in some room in the house nearly every night after dinner. So rarely do I chat with him that we've taken to communicating by calendar—leaving messages about relatives' visits or school events only in writing, not via nightly chit chats in the evenings as we used to. So keeping the work piles contained in just one part of our home is an important symbol for our fight to keep work contained in general. We can bring work out at various hours of the day, like a welcome visitor, but we want to be able to herd our responsibilities back out of sight when we want to.

Still, it's ironic that my work desk is the table where I sat with my sister and parents for so many Thanksgiving, Sunday, and Christmas dinners. My father, our town's woodshop teacher, made this drop-leaf pine table in the late 1950s. Long and thin and Shaker-style, the table stood next to the back wall of our living room, its sides folded like furled wings. On special occasions, my parents would haul it into the center of the room, raise the sides, and we'd squeeze around the easy chair and piano in order to sit down and eat. This forty- or fifty-year-old table represents the last days of a bygone era, when girls in ruffled pink dresses quietly celebrated birthdays and came to dinner when called. Now its smooth pine surface holds piles of books, folders, to-do lists, cassette tapes, and computer disks. The boundary-less, messiness of my work sits upon this table, an anchor for a boundary-less, messy new world.

These two sides of my table—the past and present, home and work—are, after all, two sides of the same coin. This unwitting pairing perhaps points to the artificiality of totally separating these halves of our lives. For the moment, I want to keep my work anchored to this table, restrained to a corner of my apartment. But it's nice having the work I love nearby, and being able to move back and forth between these so-connected worlds.

SEVEN

Beyond Four Walls:

Rediscovering and Reinventing

Home

"Make yourself at home," we say to the guest whom we invite into our dwelling. In this world of busyness, overscheduling and external pressures, it is an invitation we need also to extend to ourselves. . . .

Clare Cooper Marcus, *House as a Mirror of Self*

From the moment I started writing this book, I struggled with two questions: What is a home, and do we really need one?

Instinctively, I knew that home means more than four walls or the latest designer furniture. Home is physical but much, much more, just as people have bodies *and* the capacity to exist in a world of unlimited ideas. I knew as well, from the beginning, that home is enormously subjective. "How can you possibly write about home?" a friend asked as I began my research. "Each one is so different!" She is right. Our homes have their own distinct look, feel, and rhythm. They are utterly individual.

Still, a few core ideas of home have survived for millennia, shared by peoples around the world, often unconsciously. Just as the look of houses varies, these ideas differ by culture and era, depending on the values of the moment. At one time, homes are organized around nuclear families; in another period, relatives and acquaintances

149

commonly share domestic space. Both types of homes shelter social networks. It's as though, at any given time in history, certain genres of music attain popularity, while others fall from grace. Yet all are woven from the same system of notes.

Our idea of home is changing rapidly, and rightly so. But as we move beyond the Industrial Age and into the twenty-first century, we must take the time to look beyond our four walls and carefully think about what we seek in a home, collectively and individually. Humans always have depended on shelter for elemental reasons. What do we need to preserve from dwellings of the past? In an era of mobile technology, we want our homes to play new roles in our lives. How should we redefine the idea of home to embrace the Information Age? Perhaps more than at any other time, our society has the resources and potential to create whatever homes we wish. But first, we must decide what we value in a home.

Home is so aligned with humans and their mutability that the word itself often has been redefined through the ages. The Roman word *domus* signified not only a house, but domesticity, homeliness, even peace. It grew from the Indo-European root *dem*, meaning both family and to build. In contrast, the Greeks used the same root, *dem*, through its definition "to build" to make *domus*, their word for house. The Greek word *oikos* signified home, eventually giving us the word "economy."

Our word "house" derives from German, and its meaning hasn't changed through the ages. Just as "sea" has always meant the sea, not a harbor or an inlet, "house" has always defined a dwelling built for humans. Not until the fourteenth century did the word begin to be applied to certain public buildings, such as "ale house," or "publishing house."

Today, many European languages have no word as meaningful as the English word "home," which can signify a native country, a town of birth, one's dwelling, and more. In French and Spanish, house and home are the same: "to be at home is literally 'inside one's house.'" In this context, home is more enclosed, and less worldly.

No matter. Mostly, such etymological curiosities show us how snippets of language and their connotations metamorphose, reflecting changes in people's traditions and values. In times when the domestication of fire meant survival to a house and its occupants, the word "hearth" carried much of the weight of the word "home." Today, speaking of "hearth and home" has an old-fashioned ring. In Sweden, people still talk about summer homes, although these cottages, as in the United States, are being used more often year-round. (Perhaps facing such long winters, Swedes can't bear to give up a chance to utter a word that carries such visions of light, warmth, and play.) In contrast, Americans say they're off to their second home or vacation house, but don't speak of summer houses much anymore. Language follows and eventually reflects social trends, like a child struggling to keep up with her big sister.

We still say "home," but our vision of what this entails—emotionally, physically, socially—is slowly moving away from Industrial Age ideals. The middle-class notion of home as a separate sphere arose as paid work became centered outside residences, and as public establishments, such as schools, took over social functions formerly handled by the family. The middle classes turned away from the tradition of sharing their housing with apprentices, lodgers, and other non-family members. Women were expected to stay home to nurture this private fiefdom. This ideal didn't always reflect realities of nineteenth- and twentieth-century life. Lower-class and rural women worked outside the home, or earned money through cottage industries such as sewing. Still, the idea of the home as a private retreat held sway for almost two centuries. This is the totem we are dismantling.

I am not lamenting the past. We should leave behind many aspects of the Industrial Age, such as the notion that home is an exclusively feminine sphere. This is not because domestic activities—the care and feeding of the human race—are less important than the paid work of the wider world. The challenges of caring for a home and its dwellers are *too* important to leave to just one gender. Yet rather than expecting men to participate fully at home, both men and women are orphaning domesticity. In an era when most women work outside the home, they don't want to be saddled with the domestic burdens that imprisoned their mothers and grandmothers. And men haven't been taught to value home, the "lesser" sphere. Interestingly, major domestic reformers of the late nineteenth and early twentieth centuries didn't think to include men in their vision of progressive homes. The American writer Catharine Beecher extolled home as a shrine to female talents. German Marxist August Bebel proposed collective dining and child-care facilities in apartment buildings—run by women. In the next century, we should expect that everyone who inhabits a home should care for its survival.

Nor should we cling to a rigid ideal of a proper home as consisting of a dad, mom, and children. Demographics tell a different story, and we should listen. Just as the outpouring of women into the workplace changes our lives, so the growth of single person and single parent households, gay couples, and stepfamilies should inspire a more flexible definition of home. Anyone, collectively or individually, can create a home. Home, because of its regularity and incommensurable activities, has been called "often absurd, and often cruel." For me, home is absurd when defined by demographics or social dictates.

Home needn't be a feminine sphere, nor one properly created only by Ozzie and Harriet. But we must take care not to jettison all Industrial Age notions of home. As we enter the Information Age, we are rapidly tearing down old divisions between home and work, public and private. This trend is transforming the physical spaces, perimeters of privacy, and emotional dynamics of home. But if we fully remove the boundaries that set home apart from the wider world, that make home a refuge, we will be left exposed and alone in a world of accelerating and overwhelming change.

Recall the New York apartment of Bill Lipschutz and Lynnelle Jones, the financiers who placed monitors in sofas and niches in order keep up with global markets. Their apartment seems so space-age, yet exemplifies a trend to integrate work and home into every minute of the day. Ubiquitous computing, along with multifunctional rooms and furnishings, bring work into the heart of home. Such trends shatter the old dictate of "a time and place for everything" and infuse home with a refreshing dose of flexibility. Yet, as architect Danelle Guthrie discovered in her California WorkHouse, an absence of boundaries can leave people adrift.

We search for home in all corners of our lives.

We are struggling with the increasing permeability of home wrought by technology. Unlike the telephone, which brought outsiders into our houses one at a time, the Internet connects us to the larger world. New technologies transform our relationships from "episodic to always-on." Our ability to control the fading boundaries of home often depends on power, as my conversations with secretaries show. The result is a marketplace of privacy, where the idea of refuge holds little currency. In dismantling the boundaries of home, we risk letting important elements of our humanity—peace, privacy, intimacy—slip away.

Sensing these losses, we are seeking refuge elsewhere, imbuing spaces outside our homes with the qualities we lack within. We search for home in all corners of our lives—from the car, where we tap a concierge for help with our domestic chores; to a hotel room, where we search for the peace we can't find day-to-day; to the office, where we rest and play in a social web based on competition. We are trying out new ways to "home."

A new breed of business nomad roams the globe so ceaselessly that they essentially have no home. They might have several houses and apartments, but visits to them are so short that there isn't even time to do laundry. "Do humans need nests? That's not at all clear to me. I have a sense that this nesting thing is highly overrated," asserts Jay Ogilvy, a market researcher and business nomad. One woman is proud that she calms her six-year-old by reading a favorite book over the telephone. A businessman socializes more with workmates than family. A consultant says the 385 stamps in her passport show that she belongs all over the world, not to one place. To me, this woman belongs nowhere, and her aloneness is appalling.

In his prescient 1957 novel *Homo Faber*, Swiss architect Max Frisch tells the story of an engineer who travels so often that he gradually loses ties to home and, ultimately, to his identity. Walter Faber is so rootless that he falls in love with his own daughter, a tragedy that leads to her death. "Homo Faber's grave mistake was his conviction that man can exist without a domicile," writes Finnish architect Juhani Pallasmaa in a 1995 essay. Moreover, Faber's alienation mirrors our own, Pallasmaa observes. "We have become homeless in our culture of abundance."

These globetrotting nomads, real and fictional, lead extreme lives. Few of us have cut ties to home so completely. Our attempts to view the car or workplace as "home" are natural experiments, stemming from our newfound abilities to embrace a mobility that more than ever ignores the fetters of time and space. As I described earlier, we have much in common with the nomadic way of life that dominated human history for millennia. Our days are colored more by fluid, individualistic areas of "focus" than by inflexible sets of boundaries. We are gladly loosening rigid dictates of the Industrial Age, and seeking to be *at home* in an increasingly boundary-less world.

But to be *at home* in the world is not enough. We need a *home*. In preindustrial times, most people derived a strong sense of security from belonging to a geographic locale, a well-defined social order, and a religion. They may have been more at home in the world than in any particular house. Certainly, they lacked a home, if home is narrowly defined as a private retreat shared by nuclear family. Today, social systems and old predictabilities are loosening. Jobs are insecure and one-company careers are a rarity. Traditional rules of marriage and family are fading. Neighborhood ties are loosening. Technology weakens our ties to time and place. At least for now, we need to preserve the home—albeit a redefined, flexible, and mobile idea of home—as a place of anchor.

We must also keep home as a refuge, from the public world and from work. America, with its roots in Puritan-immigrant-pioneer values, has an enormous bias in favor of work and against private life. This collective work ethic has long made the economy hum, but has also made practically any activity except work seem downright un-American. Vacations were a creation of the Industrial Age. But "vacationing generated fear and anxiety among the nineteenth-century middle class, because vacationers were people at leisure, and leisure remained problematic," writes historian Cindy Aron. Americans of the time favored tours of factories and worksites, including the Chicago stockyards. Today, we don't watch others work while on vacation as much as we tote our own jobs along.

In preindustrial times, people combined work and home in one place, and toiled until a task was complete, as we do increasingly. Yet hundreds of years ago, church and village holidays, plus natural cues, inspired times for rest, play, and thought. In this age, a domestic refuge is our best hope for protecting a private life. This refuge need not be an inviolate sphere of domesticity. I work at home, setting up my laptop in quiet corners and at various hours, yet my home is not a workplace.

We must reinvent home, incorporating the mobility and flexibility that characterize this new age, while preserving the boundaries that give us refuge. To do so, we need to make our homes places of *experience, rootedness, learning, and sharing.*

> *A house that has been experienced is not an inert box. Inhabited space transcends geometrical space.*
>
> Gaston Bachelard

I recall reading a design book in which the author, Alexandra Stoddard, told her readers that in order to create a sense of home, they must spend time there. I was shocked, not because I disagreed with her suggestion. Rather, it amazed me that a decorator would have to say this. Her words reflect an era when people spend little time at home.

Just as cooking needn't be fancy to express care for another, so home life needn't take up all our time. But a home does take time to create. A home is *experienced*, in the words of the French philosopher Gaston Bachelard. In his book *The Poetics of Space*, he describes how the smallest of everyday actions, such as polishing a table, rejuvenate home by infusing objects with human dignity.

Other writers compare making a home to weaving, an apt analogy. Fabric is made thread by thread, bit by bit. From the sum of many tiny parts come a distinct whole. My home is the smell of cinnamon pancakes on a Saturday morning; a fleeting splash of sunshine in a lemon-yellow kitchen; whispers in the dark as two girls settle down to sleep; tears and giggles. The scent of a friend I've known all my life brings back a deeper sense of home—a return to the safety and possibility of childhood. This is a lost home, but powerful nonetheless. Memory is one of the most important threads of home.

Experience divides old from new. It is the richness we sense from being with an elder who has lived long and is comfortable in her own skin. It is the sigh of our body as we slip on a familiar sweater. It is the sensation we get when we return to a house that is truly a home.

> The notion of rootedness reflects all . . .
> aspects of home.
>
> Tomas Wikström

Home is a place, not just a time. This is increasingly easy to forget in an era when technology spirits us beyond four walls and a piece of land. If your workmates sit in Calcutta and Belfast, then why not correct your daughter's homework by fax or carry out a marriage by Palm Pilot and e-mail? More families are using technology to split up physically for parts of the week while remaining in virtual touch. But ignoring the role of "place" in human life, meaning both face-to-face contact and a shared physical location, risks a fragmentation of self and household. Virtual connections can add to relationships but cannot sustain a home.

This doesn't mean we should shun mobility. Home needn't be entirely rooted, or else it risks turning into a prison. In many cultures with a strong sense of place and home, people move regularly. Native Americans, Alpine herdsmen, and Inuits all moved seasonally, often with dwellings in tow. Today, a growing number of Americans transfer the domestic idea of refuge to a second home, together extending—but not dismantling—the boundaries of shelter. Home can be flexible, while anchored.

Architecture professor Tomas Wikström studied a group of Swedes whose apartments were undergoing an enormous renovation, inside and out. Local officials couldn't understand the tenants' dismay, since the modernization would improve their housing. But Wikström found that the repairs disturbed the residents by shaking their ties to the places they called home. The home involved many qualities—a point of return, a connection to neighborhood, a shelter from the world, a space of autonomy. Underlying all these characteristics stood a sense of rootedness, a sense of place.

The home is a craft cultivated by all its members.

Mihaly Csikszentmihalyi and Eugene Rochberg-Halton

In 1974, Csikszentmihalyi and Rochberg-Halton interviewed 300 members of 82 Chicago families to study the role of household objects in their lives. In their classic book *The Meaning of Things: Domestic Symbols and the Self*, they describe families who are warmly attached to home and to each other, and "cool" families detached from home and driven more by selfish goals. The family members create the personalities of each home. Warm families invent their homes. "The meanings that keep these families together are woven and mended by the constant attention of those who comprise them," the authors observe. This contrasts with the idea of the traditional family, which is held together by rigid social forces and therefore may be closely knit but is not always warm.

The invention of home involves learning, modeling, and experimentation, both individually and as a group. Many of the people I interviewed for this book who had created a flexible, even mobile refuge did so by trial and error.

Danelle Guthrie and Tom Buresh, Colin Ochel, Jim and
Maddy Hanlon, and Jan Monti all thought about home,
tinkered with different ways of having one, and spent time
weaving their home, sometimes with great effort. This
process is particularly crucial to children, for whom the
home is a first school.

The process of learning and invention makes home
much more than a place to live. Through invention, home
becomes a repository of life, as one man noted in an online
newsletter devoted to debating technology's impact on
people. In response to a technologist touting appliances that
tell the user how to cook, Phil Walsh wrote why he doesn't
want a computer involved in the creation of his wife's
favorite dish, lasagna with béchamel sauce. (Even those
who don't like cooking should consider his words.) After
combining butter, flour, and cream on the stove, Walsh must
heat the sauce so it thickens, but not so much that it burns—
a challenge that takes skill and practice.

> Putting this dish in front of my family, having
> them ooh and aah, and having my wife pronounce
> it the best thing she's ever eaten brings me
> satisfaction. No small part of that satisfaction
> stems directly from knowing that dish successfully
> requires skills I had to work to develop.

> [The technologist] believes my life will be in some
> way better if he provides me with a pan that will
> tell me when the béchamel sauce is scorching.
> What his "wondrous" pan really does is rob me of
> an opportunity to live (because that's what trying
> and failing and learning and trying again until you
> get it right really is), and it's too bad if we continue
> to rush toward a place where living is apparently
> viewed as too much of an inconvenience to be
> tolerated.

*Communicating with each other was the first
and most important theme in the experience of
pleasantness.*

Paul J. J. Pennartz

A house is for sharing. This seems odd to say at a time when more than a quarter of households consist of one person, and nearly thirty percent of children live with one parent, up from twelve percent in 1970. But a home cannot be defined by the number of its occupants, anymore than a house can be valued by size alone.

Even for those living alone, a house must be a place of sharing. If we create a home just for ourselves, we lose the crucial human quality of sociability. Growing up in our small town, my sister and I spent much time visiting a family friend who was a teacher. It never occurred to me that she lived alone, partly because she truly was a member of our family. Her home was a sharing place as well. Her former students often stopped by, and she kept treats just for us. She had kept a stock of the little cocktail napkins you'd never buy just for yourself, for the nights she played bridge or for times when teachers came over. She created a comfortable home and shared it.

Within a home, a family that doesn't share with each other is sheltered yet homeless. In his study of how homes are experienced, sociologist Paul Pennartz asked what creates atmosphere—the size of rooms, the time of day, the activity? Foremost, he found that a pleasant atmosphere depends on household communications, meaning both shared activities and people's availability to one another. Without sharing, we—and our homes—are islands.

I did not intend to write a book about home. For four years, I wrote articles about work, from the trials of night shifts to the risks of office romances. The workplace beat was hot. No newspaper or magazine has a "home" correspondent, except those who cover furniture and design, the stuff of houses, not homes.

But as the worlds of home and work began to blur and the lines between public and private started to fade, I realized that I needed to think more about home. It's the side of the coin that is constantly ignored. Home is intimately tied up with the revolutionary changes we're experiencing in men's and women's roles, and in the ways we work. That's one reason why home has such political and visceral connotations today. Home remains a powerful subject simply because it matters so much. Just as experience, rootedness, learning, and sharing are the building blocks of home, so home is a cornerstone of humanity. We ignore the importance of home only at the risk of harming the fabric of our society.

In their study of household objects, Csikszentmihalyi and Rochberg-Halton found that "warm" families, who felt positively about home and cared for one another, participated in school, professional, community, and political groups much more often than "cool" families did. Warm family members admired public figures and creative people. Cool families admired each other, and took part in fewer activities outside the home. Their participation was limited mainly to athletic and religious organizations. Children from cool homes almost exclusively joined sports teams. The message is clear: the attention family members give to the home and each other frees them to invest energy in community goals. Reading this study, I recalled Cheryl Mendelson, author of the best-selling housekeeping manual, who told me that keeping house is integral to the very foundation of a democratic society. How can citizens govern themselves if they can't even take care of themselves and their homes?

I see signs that people are ready to think more about home. As Americans begin a new century, they are worn out. Many profited from the high-flying 1990s economy, but paid a heavy social and emotional toll for their gains. People had little opportunity for family, private time, moments of thought, even sleep. The headlines are telling: "Start-up Attracts Staff With a Ban on Midnight Oil," "Taking the Offensive Against Cell Phones." Sixty-five percent of workers ages twenty-one to sixty-five would give up pay for more time with families, a recent poll found. More than seventy percent of men ages twenty-one to thirty-nine would do so. More dramatically, nearly eighty-five percent of those polled prefer distinct boundaries between work and private life.

As we begin the Information Age, we cannot go backward. Technology is slowly eroding the Industrial Age inventions of the eight-hour workday, the weekend, and the vacation. The old rules surrounding work and family, public and private are broken, yet we will be struggling for many years, perhaps decades, to discover the new patterns of society. We feel betwixt and between, as I did when I found myself bringing work home so that I could see my children, then brusquely herding them to bed so that I could return to work. To the first two questions I posed as I began this book—what is a home, and do we need one—I must add a third: how do we find home today?

On the drizzling January day when I visited Swedish physicist Bodil Jönsson, she offered a simple lifeline for those drowning in their own busyness and hurryings: make up your mind. In other words, you must decide whether you want to splinter yourself via cell phone, or give those in your presence the gift of your full attention. You can decide to take the time to tackle a difficult project, or fritter your days away with mundane chores. Jönsson's challenge reminds us that we can regain control of our lives in a fast-paced, high-tech, confusing age.

To create a home, you must make up your mind. Jeffrey Lutzner, who runs a Philadelphia business making doors and windows, reworked his career so he could spend time with his children and share the work of home equally with his wife. He deliberately made the time and place for home. "Friends tell me that I'm lucky because I have a business that allows me to do this," he says. "Well, am I really just lucky? Or am I smart enough to recognize that this is how business can be done?" To create a home, you must experiment, and make the time to forge a sheltering place that is giving and thoughtful. This is not easy, and there are no rule books for this task. But if you don't take the time and effort to try, you may be housed, but homeless.

In creating a home, perhaps some will find refuge in a second house, framed by the comforting immutability of landscape, or in a room that is deliberately kept for togetherness, not for the chaos of a "roommate society." Others might simply set aside time to eat together, uninterrupted by television and telephone. Sometimes, I make a private goal that all four members of my family will do something on a weekend we've never done together before. The novelty of this moment contains both a beginning and a restoration of all that home means.

Day by day, home is a place of going out, and returning. In each of our lives, home is inextricably tied to the cycles of beginnings and endings that mark our passage on earth. Home is found in the most mundane tasks of survival, and in the core questions of what it means to be human. Isn't it time that we thought more about home?

Diary Epilogue: Thinking Out Loud

In writing this diary, I've been thinking out loud—on paper. I've filled three notebooks with my questions, confusion, observations, and ideas about my home and the changing nature of home in the twenty-first century. I've spilled my thoughts liberally on paper, and then picked up a few shards of the resulting heart, soul, or rationale to share with you.

These diary entries are snapshots of a messy, sometimes accidental work-in-progress. But these fragments are telling. Just as the larger questions of life, work, identity, and love get played out on the smallest of scales, so these diaries capture the seeming trivialities that represent core ideas of home: the irony of working on the table where I ate Christmas dinner as a child; the angst of fixing a filling supper on a work night; the relief of turning off a cell phone to enjoy a walk home at sunset. Maybe my own foibles and experiments will inspire you to think about the telling details of your home life.

Put together, and with hindsight, these diaries chronicle my evolution in work styles from the Industrial Age to the Computer Age. I had always worked at home, yet fearfully preserved a huge gulf between my home and my job. While writing this book, I learned the importance of keeping boundaries between home and work, public and private, here and there. But I learned how to make and remake these boundaries, cross and recross between these two worlds without turning my life into a jumble.

Where does that leave me now? Perhaps in much the same place as I started from—wondering how often to hurry my children to bed so I can write; questioning whether to leave my cell phone on while accompanying my daughter to a birthday party. In this age, we always may have more questions than answers about home, as we individually redefine our ideas of refuge, domesticity, home-work, privacy. At the moment, I'm faced with the looming question of whether to take apart my "home office" and recapture my bedroom. (To my husband's chagrin, I'm leaning toward paring down but keeping this workspace.) As I complete this book, I'm wondering whether I'll feel free to do a domestic chore from work on a slow news day. (I like to think I will.) Whatever happens, I know that this diary cannot help me tie up such dilemmas into neat packages, solved once and for all. Nor can this book do that for you.

Then again, I'll never look at my worktable, dinner hour, dining room table, laptop, or children's bedtime in the same way. Rather than simply living in my home, I've learned to think about my home. In writing this diary and this book, I've discovered a crucial part of the world that I'd hardly given deep consideration.

We are all pioneers in the re-creation of home. We should all have a say in this challenge. We should all start thinking out loud about home, perhaps in a conversation with a spouse, a daydream one afternoon, an e-mail to a friend, a private journal, or while reading a book. I'll keep thinking about home, experimenting with home, creating and re-creating a home as long as I live. Even if you find your home, your searching is not done.

Notes

Author's Note: Unless otherwise indicated, people quoted in the book were interviewed by the author.

Introduction

1. Certainly, there always will. . . . Christena E. Nippert-Eng, *Home and Work: Negotiating Boundaries Through Everyday Life* (Chicago: The University of Chicago Press, 1995), 6 and 23.

2. Zoologist Edward O. Wilson. . . . Thomas Petzinger, Jr., "Futurology: Talking About Tomorrow," *The Wall Street Journal*, 31 December 1999, R16.

3. In Mehinacu Indian villages. . . . Irwin Altman, "Privacy Regulation: Culturally Universal or Culturally Specific," *Journal of Social Issues* 33, no. 3 (1977): 72-74.

1. The Architecture of Home-Work

1. The things that surround. . . . Mihaly Csikszentmihalyi and Eugene Rochberg-Halton, *The Meaning of Things: Domestic Symbols and the Self* (Cambridge, UK: Cambridge University Press, 1981), 16.

2. Enter the New York. . . . "Style with Elsa Klensch," Cable News Network, 24 July 1999.

3. I often trade all. . . . Charles Gandee, "Open House," *Vogue*, July 1999, 188.

4. It's the fastest growing. . . . Telephone interview with Kelly Cain, senior vice-president of product development at Stanley Furniture, 2 November 1999.

5. Studies show that a. . . . "Project Blur," Greenfield Online Inc., February 2000. Also "Home Office Trends: A Report of How Offices Are Being Used and How They Are Furnished and Equipped," No. 9021, Wirthlin Worldwide, June 1998, 8-9.

6. For e-mailing in bed. . . in classrooms. Dan Shaw, "Domestic Bliss: Laptop of Luxury," *House & Garden*, September 1999, 63-64.

7. Computing belongs in furniture. . . . Vision statement of "Things That Think" department at MIT Media Lab, web site: www.media.mit.edu/ttt/vision.html.

8. "Invisibility is the missing. . . . Neil Gershenfeld, *When Things Start to Think* (New York: Henry Holt and Company, 1999), 7.

9. "Pages other than the. . . . Gershenfeld, 18.

10. Bill Buxton, a professor. . . . William Buxton, "Living in Augmented Reality: Ubiquitous Media and Reactive Environments," in K. Finn, A. Sellen, and S. Wilbur, eds., *Video-Mediated Communication* (Mahwah, NJ: Lawrence Erlbaum Associates, 1997), 363-384.

11. By the seventeenth century. . . . Witold Rybczynski, *Home: A Short History of an Idea* (New York: Penguin Books, 1987), 39.

12. When IBM paired with. . . . Maggie Jackson, "Living over the Store, Vacationing with Laptop: Blending Home and Work," *The Associated Press*, 25 July 1999.

13. In the accompanying catalog. . . . Terence Riley, *The Un-Private House* (New York: The Museum of Modern Art, 1999), 11 and 28.

14. One builder's house features. . . . Linda Sandler, "If It's Tuesday, This Must Be the Living Room," *The Wall Street Journal*, 25 June 1999, W10.

15. Just before The Museum. . . . Riley, 24.

2. Private Lives

1. "An important reason that. . . . *Summit* magazine, 1993.

2. "At its best, privacy. . . . Janna Malamud Smith, *Private Matters: In Defense of the Personal Life* (Reading, MA: Addison-Wesley, 1997), 24-25.

3. "Life was a public. . . . Witold Rybczynski, *Home: A Short History of an Idea* (New York: Penguin Books, 1987), 35.

4. "Home became a refuge. . . . Christena E. Nippert-Eng, *Home and Work: Negotiating Boundaries Through Everyday Life* (Chicago: The University of Chicago Press, 1995), 19.

5. One furor arose because. . . . Bob Tedeschi, "Critics Press Legal Assault on Tracking of Web Users," *The New York Times*, 7 February 2000, C1. Also Heather Green, "Privacy: Outrage on the Web," *Business Week*, 14 February 2000, 38-39.

6. Some health-related web. . . . Jeri Clausing, "Health Web Sites Fail to Keep Personal Data Private, Study Finds," *The New York Times*, 2 February 2000, A19.

7. Chefs now use computers. . . . Amanda Hesser, "Every Bite You Take, They'll Be Watching You," *The New York Times*, 1 March 2000, F1.

8. And now video screens. . . . Dave Carpenter, "The New Muzak—Elevators Display News, Traffic, Stocks," *The Associated Press*, 7 February 2000.

9. In a seminal *Harvard*. . . . Louis Brandeis and Samuel Warren, "The Right of Privacy," *Harvard Law Review*, 4 (1890), 193.

10. A national study by. . . . Ellen Galinsky, James T. Bond, and Stacy S. Kim, "Feeling Overworked: When Work Becomes Too Much" (New York: Families and Work Institute, 2001), 29-30.

11. The secretaries I talked. . . . Jan Wahl, *Cats and Robbers* (New York: Tambourine Books, 1995).

12. The more mobile a. . . . David Caldwell and James L. Koch, "Mobile Computing and Its Impact on the Changing Nature of Work and Organizations," Santa Clara University's Center for Science, Technology and Society, 1999. Available at www.scu.edu.

13. "In today's workplace, we've. . . . Beth Sawi, speech to The Conference Board and Families and Work Institute Conference, "Work-Life 2000: Past, Present and Future," 15 March 2000.

14. "The borders between action. . . . Gary Marx, "The Declining Significance of Traditional Borders (and the

Appearance of New Borders) in an Age of High Technology," in P. Drogue, *Intelligent Environments* (Elsevier Science, 1997), 484-494.

15. Ford and Delta, the. . . . Keith Bradsher, "Ford Offers Its Workers PCs and Internet for $5 a Month," *The New York Times*, 4 February 2000, A1.

16. One thing is clear. . . . Greg Miller and Stuart Silverstein, "Even Corporate Perks Join the Dot-Com Revolution," *Los Angeles Times*, 5 February 2000, A1.

17. Armed with a court. . . . Susan Carey, "Northwest Air Probes PCs of Attendants," *The Wall Street Journal*, 10 February 2000, A3. Michael J. McCarthy, "Data Raid: In Airline's Suit, PC Becomes Legal Pawn, Raising Privacy Issues," *The Wall Street Journal*, 24 May 2000, A1. Also interviews with Northwest spokeswoman Kathy Peach and a flight attendants' lawyer, Paul Levy.

18. We have the ability. . . . Jeffrey Rosen, *The Unwanted Gaze: The Destruction of Privacy in America* (New York: Random House, 2000), 25.

19. "We will increasingly face. . . . William J. Mitchell, *e-topia: "Urban Life, Jim—But Not as We Know It"* (Cambridge, MA: The MIT Press, 1999), 117.

20. Taking this trend a. . . . Lisa Guernsey, "Now, A Few Words From Friends and Sponsors," *The New York Times*, 3 February 2000, G3.

21. I first started talking. . . . Estimates from Cahners In-Stat Group, Vice President of Research Mark Kirstein, 19 March 2001.

22. True Tech, a Dutch company. . . . Telephone interview with company spokesman Michael Erkelens, 1 February 2000.

23. This dance of accessibility. . . . J. A. English-Lueck, "Technology and Social Change: The Effects on Family and Community," speech to COSSA Congressional Seminar, 19 June 1998. Available at: www.sjsu.edu/depts/anthropology/svcp.

24. Stephen L. Talbott, editor. . . . Steve Talbott, "Privacy in an Age of Data (Part 2)," *NetFuture*, no. 29, 17 October 1996.

25. *Metropolis* magazine found a. . . . Akiko Busch, "Geography of Home," *Metropolis*, 13, no. 9 May 1994: 99 and 103.

3. Orphaning Domesticity

1. It is not in. . . . Cheryl Mendelson, *Home Comforts: The Art and Science of Keeping House* (New York: Scribner, 1999), 8.

2. A majority of women. . . . Sue Shellenbarger, "The Heralded Return of Traditional Families Is Not What It Seems," *The Wall Street Journal*, 31 May 2000, B1.

3. One day, I saw. . . . Carolynn Carreno, "Confessions of a Closet Homemaker," *The New York Times Magazine*, 30 April 2000, 132.

4. "Our homes are the. . . . Mendelson, 14.

5. In Medieval Europe, home. . . . John R. Gillis, *A World of Their Own Making: Myth, Ritual, and the Quest for Family Values* (New York: Basic Books, 1996), 24 and 32-37.

6. Colonial households, too, reflected. . . . Stephanie Coontz, *The Social Origins of Private Life: A History of American Families, 1600-1900* (London: Verso, 1991), 75-79 and 93-101.

7. In 1965, women kept. . . . John P. Robinson and Geoffrey Godbey, *Time for Life: The Surprising Ways Americans Use Their Time*, 2nd ed. (University Park, PA: The Pennsylvania State University Press, 1999), 103-105.

8. Men are doing more. . . . Arlie Hochschild with Anne Machung, *The Second Shift: Working Parents and the Revolution at Home* (New York: Viking Penguin, 1989), 4.

9. One nineteenth-century researcher. . . . Susan Strasser, *Never Done: A History of American Housework* (New York: Pantheon Books, 1982), 86-87.

10. "Tainted water supplies, rancid. . . . Strasser, 9.

11. Between 1995 and 2000. . . . "The Survey of American Consumers," 2000 Fall, MediaMark Research, Inc., New York. Also Ameripoll 82, Maritz Marketing Research, November 1999.

12. Demand is growing for. . . . Information from the U.S. Personal Chef Association, 9 May 2001.

13. Sales of prepared Thanksgiving. . . . Kortney Stringer, "Takeout Turkey on More Tables as Cooks Relax," *The Wall Street Journal*, 24 November 2000, A11.

14. Returning home each day. . . . John Demos, *Past, Present, and Personal: The Family and the Life Course in American History* (New York: Oxford University Press, 1986), 50-51.

15. Why should we try. . . . Ellen Richards, "Domestic Industries: In or Out—Why Not?" *Sixth Annual Conference on Home Economics* (Lake Placid, NY, 1904), 28.

16. Yet early on, home. . . . Sarah Stage and Virginia B. Vincenti, eds. *Rethinking Home Economics: Women and the History of a Profession* (Ithaca, NY: Cornell University Press, 1997), 2-4. Also Clifford Edward Clark, Jr., *The American Family Home*: 1800-1960 (Chapel Hill, NC: The University of North Carolina Press, 1986), 159-162.

17. No longer mandatory in. . . . Elizabeth Austin, "Saving the Home from Martha Stewart," *Washington Monthly*, 1 December 1999, 9.

18. One national study found. . . . Ellen Galinsky, *Ask the Children: What America's Children Really Think About Working Parents* (New York: William Morrow and Co., 1999), 73-77.

19. Meanwhile, the number of. . . . Leslie Berger, "What Children Do When Home and Alone," *The New York Times*, 11 April 2000, F8.

20. A great deal of. . . . Telephone interviews with Karen Tanner-Oliphant of Roselle, NJ, 25 April 2000; Sharon Gandy of Maryland Cooperative Extension at the University of Maryland, 9 May 2000; Kathy Saladino of Bellport, New York, 9 May 2000; Virginia B. Vincenti, 10

May 2000; Ann Chadwick, executive director of the Association of Family and Consumer Sciences, 11 May 2000.

21. "Around nine or ten. . . . Hofferth quoted in Leslie Berger.

22. A study of thirty. . . . Elaine Bell Kaplan, "Using Food as a Metaphor for Care: Middle-School Kids Talk About Family, School and Class Relationships," *Journal of Contemporary Ethnography* 29, no. 4 (2000): 474-509.

23. David Elkind, author of. . . . David Elkind, Ties That Stress: *The New Family Imbalance* (Cambridge, MA: Harvard University Press, 1994), 1-3 and 58.

24. Equipping kids with beepers. . . . Seven percent of households with children make a cell phone accessible to children, according to Ken Hyers of Cahners In-Stat Group. Telephone interview, 23 May 2000.

25. Kathy Peel advises families. . . . Lee Stratton, "Consider Running the Family Like a Business," *The Columbus Dispatch*, 26 January 1998, B3.

26. In this new world. . . . Elkind, 119.

27. One New Jersey teacher. . . . Telephone interview with Carol Otis, 27 April 2000.

28. We will continue to. . . . Jagdish Sheth et al., *Customer Behavior: Consumer Behavior and Beyond* (Fort Worth, TX: The Dryden Press of Harcourt Brace College Publishers, 1999), 575.

29. At that time, the. . . . Janice W. Rutherford, "An Uncommon Life," *Old House Journal*, September/October 1999, 4.

30. Our greatest enemy is. . . . Frederick, quoted in Stage and Vincenti, 25.

31. For an article I. . . . Maggie Jackson, "Generation X Is Bold, Quick, Computer-Savvy; Companies Learning to Cope," *The Associated Press*, 27 January 1999.

32. In seventeenth-century Holland. . . . Witold Rybczynski, *Home: A Short History of an Idea* (New York: Penguin Books, 1987), 72-74.

4. Creating a Home at Work

1. Employers from start-ups. . . . Maggie Jackson, "Is Your Company Your New Hometown?" *The Associated Press,* 29 September 1998.

2. These Industrial Age towns. . . . Margaret Crawford, *Building the Workingman's Paradise: The Design of American Company Towns* (London: Verso, 1995), 2.

3. With its wide boulevards. . . . Stanley Buder, *Pullman: An Experiment in Industrial Order and Community Planning, 1880-1930* (New York: Oxford University Press, 1967), 55-56 and 61-62.

4. George Pullman chose the. . . . "Amusements: A Description of the Beautiful New Opera House at Pullman," *Daily Inter Ocean*, 25 November, 1882, 14.

5. Residents were reminded to. . . . Buder, 95.

6. Eight decades before Pullman . . . on holidays. Crawford, 15-17.

7. The strict rules in. . . . Tamara K. Hareven, *Family Time and Industrial Time: The Relationship Between the Family and Work in a New England Industrial Community* (Cambridge, England: Cambridge University Press, 1982), 55.

8. In 1843, owner Benjamin. . . . John R. Commons, *A Documentary History of American Industrial Society* (Cleveland, 1910), 7: 50-51, quoted in Norman Ware, *The Industrial Worker, 1840-1860: The Reaction of American Industrial Society to the Advance of the Industrial Revolution* (Boston: Houghton Mifflin, 1924; reprinted, Chicago: Elephant Paperbacks, 1990), 35.

9. In 1829, Massachusetts mill. . . . G. Kulik, R. Parks, and T. Penn, *The New England Mill Village, 1790-1860* (Cambridge, MA: MIT Press, 1982), 298.

10. The vast Amoskeag Corporation. . . . Tamara K. Hareven and Randolph Langenbach, *Amoskeag: Life and Work in an American Factory City* (New York: Pantheon Books, 1978), 15.

11. "The Amoskeag was a. . . . Hareven and Langenbach, 233.

12. By the 1920s, many. . . . Hareven, *Family Time and Industrial Time*, 63-64.

13. "I felt like a. . . . Hareven and Langenbach, 145.

14. Some Pullman residents reveled. . . . Buder, 95-96.

15. So powerful and inescapable. . . . Hareven and Langenbach, 11.

16. Believing his roles as. . . . Buder, 154-156.

17. It is the workplace. . . . Alan Wolfe, *One Nation, After All* (New York: Viking, 1998), 233.

18. It's a quiet December. . . . Author interviews. Also Matthew DeBord, "Spin City: Studios Architecture's Offices for a Manhattan Record Company Takes It Easy," *Interiors* 159, no. 7 (July 2000), 48-53. The record company refuses to be named.

19. The designers at Studios. . . . Interview with spokeswoman Simone Rothman, 16 December 2000.

20. Recognizing these changes, office. . . . Matt Steinglass, "Post-Cubist: How a Hip, Young Turkish Designer Is Breaking Down the Square American Office System," *Metropolis*, 19, no. 4 November 1999: 99-103, 166-169.

21. With Americans working an. . . . James T. Bond, Ellen Galinsky, and Jennifer Swanberg, *The 1997 National Study of the Changing Workforce* (New York: Families and Work Institute), 71.

22. Americans on average belong. . . . Thomas Guterbock and John Fries, "Maintaining America's Social Fabric: The AARP Survey of Civic Involvement," American Association of Retired Persons, December 1997.

23. In the mid-1970s. . . . Robert Putnam, *Bowling Alone: The Collapse and Revival of American Community* (New York: Simon and Schuster, 2000), 61.

24. Only twenty percent of people. . . . Yankelovich Partners, "Yankelovich Monitor 1997," 109.

25. "It's almost as if. . . . Unnamed suburbanite quoted in Wolfe, 251.

26. Nobody regards Pullman as. . . . Richard T. Ely, "Pullman: A Social Study," *Harper's Monthly* LXX, No. 417 (1885): 463.

27. Relations with peers at. . . . Wolfe, 259-260.

28. As author Laura Nash. . . . Laura L. Nash, "The Nanny Corporation," *Across the Board: The Conference Board Magazine* 31, no. 7 (July/August 1994): 17-22.

29. Not too long ago. . . . Jeffrey Seglin, "Playing It the Company Way, After Hours," *The New York Times*, 20 February 2000, Sect. 3/4.

30. Worker housing remained filled. . . . Buder, 81-2 and 117.

31. When Richard Ely, a. . . . Ely, 463.

32. If we grow too. . . . Laura Nash is eloquent on this point. See also her article "The Virtual Job," *The Wilson Quarterly* 18, no. 4 (1994): 72-81.

5. Home-ing

1. One new car can. . . . Dan Lienert, "Add Rats and Snakes and Play 'Survivor,'" *The New York Times*, 17 September 2000, Sect. 12, 1.

2. "The tendency of the. . . . Anna McClure Sholl, "The House," *Atlantic Monthly* 98, no. 5 (1 November 1906): 693-697.

3. Although only about six. . . . "Second Homes-Recreational Property," National Association of Realtors report. 9 May 2000, 1. Sales of second homes rose from 296,000 in 1995 to 377,000 in 1999, a 27.4 percent increase. There are an estimated 6.1 million second homes in the United States.

4. Nearly one in three. . . . "The American Recreational Property Survey: 1999," The American Resort Development Association, June 1999, 6.

5. Interest in second homes. . . . "National Leisure Travel Monitor 2000," Yesewich, Pepperdine and Brown/Yankelovich Partners.

6. E. B. White captured the. . . . E. B. White, "Once More to the Lake," in *One Man's Meat* (New York: Harper & Brothers, 1938, 1944), 250.

7. A half century later. . . . Amy Willard Cross, *The Summer House: A Tradition of Leisure* (New York: Harper Collins, 1992), 98.

8. Perhaps most telling of. . . . Blaine Harden, "Summer Residents Want Year-Round Voice," *The New York Times*, 30 May 2000, A1.

9. As researcher Christena Nippert-Eng. . . . Christena Nippert-Eng, *Home and Work: Negotiating Boundaries Through Everyday Life* (Chicago: University of Chicago Press, 1995), 27.

10. Nearly all the thirty. . . . Davina Chaplin,"Consuming Work/Productive Leisure: The Consumption Patterns of Second Home Environments," *Leisure Studies* 18, no. 1 (1999), 51.

11. "There is no need. . . . Pliny the Younger, Epistles V.vi.45, quoted in James S. Ackerman, *The Villa: Form and Ideology of Country Houses* (Princeton, NJ: Princeton University Press, 1990), 13.

12. In 1559, when Giuseppe. . . . Giuseppe Falcone, *La Nuova, Vaga et Dilettevole Villa*, Brescia, 1559, quoted in Ackerman, 112.

13. *House Beautiful* reported in. . . . John Ingersoll, "Vacation Home Living," *House Beautiful*, 112 (August 1970), 52.

14. Following Durant's style, summer. . . . Cross, 180.

15. For one, they are. . . . National Association of Realtors report, 2.

16. Ancient Romans looked to. . . . Ackerman, 60-61. Also Agostino Gallo, *La Dieci Giornate della vera agricoltura et piacori della villa* (Brescia 1564), 125-126, quoted in Ackerman, 117-118.

17. There is, in particular. . . William Mitchell, *e-topia: "Urban Life, Jim—But Not as We Know It"* (Cambridge, MA: The MIT Press, 1999), 73.

18. In 1968, urbanist Melvin. . . . Melvin Webber, "The Post-City Age," *Daedulus* 97 (1968), 1091-1110, quoted in Mitchell, 75-76.

19. "We can expect then. . . . Mitchell, 76.

20. Home Is Where You. . . . Ford press release, 19 April 2000.

21. Marjorie Ryan, a mother. . . . Patrick Kennedy, "Not Your Ordinary Autos," *Minneapolis-St. Paul Star-Tribune,* 1 September 2000, D1.

22. A general contractor, tired. . . . Charlotte Mulhern, "Desk a Go-Go," *Home Office Magazine,* January/February 1998, 49.

23. "Something domestic, as in. . . . Giles Felton, "A Place for Everything Under the Sun-Roof," *The New York Times,* 17 May 2000, Automobiles Section, 6.

24. The yearning for home. . . . "Fractional Ownership Becoming More Popular in Resort Towns," *The Associated Press,* 28 August 2000.

25. Travelers of all sorts. . . . Interview with Bjorn Hanson, senior executive with PricewaterhouseCoopers, 2 October 2000.

26. In many nomadic hunter/gatherer. . . . Peter J. Wilson, *The Domestication of the Human Species* (New Haven, CT: Yale University Press, 1988), 30 and 50.

27. With the institution of. . . . Wilson, 64.

28. In ancient Greece a. . . . Hannah Arendt, *The Human Condition* (Chicago: University of Chicago Press, 1958), 29-30.

29. Home allows us to. . . . Olivier Marc, *Psychology of the House* (London: Thames and Hudson, 1977), 14.

30. "Incessant occupation is not. . . . Charlotte Perkins Gilman, *The Home, Its Work and Influence* (New York: McClure, Phillips and Co., 1903), 338.

6. *Ett Hem* (A Home)

1. Dirt-poor Sweden didn't. . . . Kurt Samuelsson, *From Great Power to Welfare State: 300 Years of Swedish Social Development* (London: Allen & Unwin, 1968), 165-166.

2. More than half of. . . . "Telecommunications and Information Technology in Sweden" (Stockholm: Swedish Institute, 2000), 1. For information on mobile phones, see "Sweden Seeks Utopia From Tech Boom," *The Wall Street Journal,* 17 July 2000, A1.

3. Before I arrived, a. . . . Kerstin Kåll, "A Home," *BrainHeart Magazine*, June 2000, 22-23.

4. Beginning in the 1970s. . . . "Telecommunications and Information Technology in Sweden," 1.

5. By 2000, media and. . . . Stryker McGuire, "Shining Stockholm," *Newsweek* European edition, 7 February 2000, 52-59.

6. But nowadays, even outside. . . . Dominique Anxo et al., "Time, Lifestyles and Transitions in France and Sweden," in O'Reilly, J. et al., eds., *Working-Time Changes: Social Integration Through Transitional Labour Markets* (Cheltenham: Edward Elgar, 2000).

7. In 1997, nearly sixty. . . . *Women and Men in Sweden: Facts and Figures 1998* (Stockholm: Statistics Sweden, 1998), 58. About fifty-five percent of Americans felt sometimes or often overworked in the past three months, according to Ellen Galinsky, James T. Bond, and Stacy S. Kim, "Feeling Overworked: When Work Becomes Too Much" (New York: Families and Work Institute, 2001), 14-15.

8. And as in the. . . . *Women and Men in Sweden: Facts and Figures 2000* (Stockholm: Statistics Sweden, 2000), 3. In 1970, sixty percent of Swedish women of working age were in the labor market.

9. Spray's sprawling offices are. . . . Figures from Torbjörn Bengtsson, IT project manager for Business Area Stockholm, a government investment group, 15 March 2001.

10. If Stockholm is, according. . . . Paul Saffo, director of the Institute of the Future, Menlo Park, CA, quoted in McGuire, 59.

11. When I mentioned reading. . . . Elizabeth Bernstein, "The Disappearing Kitchen," *The Wall Street Journal*, 12 January 2001, W1.

12. "The kitchen table is. . . . Ulla Westerberg, "Dwelling Habits and Values—Inertia and Change in Sweden," in J. Teklenburg, J. van Andel, J. Smeets, A. Seidel, eds., *Shifting Balances, Changing Roles in Policy, Research and Design, Proceedings of the 15th Bi-Annual Conference of the*

International Association for People-Environment Studies (European Institute of Retailing and Service Studies, 1998).

13. "Especially families with children. . . . Westerberg, "Dwelling Habits and Values."

14. Kabel's consumer interviews and. . . . "Electrolux Screenfridge Premieres Today in 50 Danish Homes," press release by E2 Home, Business Wire, 8 September 2000. Carol J. Williams, "'Smart Appliances' to Usher in Jetson-Like Households," *Los Angeles Times*, 1 January 2000, A2.

15. The home became a. . . . Michelle Facos, "Definitely Swedish: Carl Larsson's Home in Sundborn," *Scandinavian Review* 81, no. 2 (1993), 63.

16. "This complex local economy. . . . David Popenoe, *Disturbing the Nest: Family Change and Decline in Modern Societies* (New York: Aldine de Gruyter, 1988), 86.

17. About one in twelve. . . . Hans-Ingvar Johnsson, trans. Victor Kayfetz, *Spotlight on Sweden: The Country and Its People,* second ed. (Stockholm: The Swedish Institute, 1999), 223.

18. Traveling across Sweden in. . . . Robert Colton, *Rambles in Sweden and Gottland* (London: Richard Bentley, 1847), 267 and 120-122.

19. "Lilla Hyttnäs underwent constant. . . . Facos, 63.

20. Again and again, the. . . . Facos, 63-64.

21. Most Swedish homes of. . . . Orvar Löfgren, "The Sweetness of Home: Class, Culture and Family Life in Sweden," *Ethnologia Europaea* 14 (1984), 46-48.

22. Observers from Larsson's day. . . . O. G. von Heidenstam, *Swedish Life in Town and Country* (New York: G.P. Putnam's Sons, The Knickerbocker Press, 1904), 35 and 216.

23. "For in Sweden," von. . . . von Heidenstam, 74-75.

24. In 1904, Stockholm's 300,000. . . . Stockholm population found in *Encyclopedia Britannica* 1969, s.v. "Stockholm." New York population figure found in *World Almanac* 1929, s.v. "New York City population."

25. "If you eliminate the. . . . Jarret Adams, "In the Shadow of Finland: In Stockholm, a Wireless Klondike Paves a Future for the Swedes," *Red Herring*, October 2000, 322.

26. Eighty percent of Swedish. . . . Interview with Henrik Pålsson, ConsumerLab Director, Ericsson Mobile Communications AB, 15 January 2001.

27. Nearly every person I. . . . In the United States, Jönsson's book is titled *Unwinding the Clock* (New York: Harcourt, 2001).

7. Beyond Four Walls

1. "Make yourself at home. . . . Clare Cooper Marcus, *House as a Mirror of Self* (Berkeley, CA: Conari Press, 1995), 18.

2. The Roman word *domus*. . . . Joseph Rykwert, "House and Home," in Arien Mack, ed., *Home: A Place in the World* (New York: New York University Press, 1993), 48.

3. Our word "house" derives. . . . John Hollander, "It All Depends," in Mack, 40.

4. Today, many European languages. . . . David E. Sopher, "The Landscape of Home: Myth, Experience, Social Meaning" in D. W. Meinig, ed., *The Interpretation of Ordinary Landscapes: Geographical Essays* (New York: Oxford University Press, 1979), 130.

5. Interestingly, major domestic reformers. . . . Dolores Hayden, *Redesigning the American Dream: The Future of Housing, Work, and Family Life* (New York: W.W. Norton and Company, 1984), 74.

6. Home, because of its. . . . Mary Douglas, "The Idea of Home: A Kind of Space," in Mack, 279.

7. New technologies transform our. . . . Phil Agre, "Welcome to the Always-On World," *IEEE Spectrum 38*, no. 1 (2001): 10, 13.

8. "Do humans need nests? . . . not to one place. Joel Garreau, "Home Is Where the Phone Is: Roaming Legion of High-Tech Nomads Takes Happily to Ancient Path," *The Washington Post*, 17 October 2000, A1.

9. In his prescient 1957. . . . Max Frisch, *Homo Faber*, Michael Bullock, trans. (n.p.: Suhrkamp Verlag, 1957; reprint, London: Eyre Methuen, 1974).

10. "Homo Faber's grave mistake. . . . Juhani Pallasmaa, "Identity, Intimacy and Domicile: Notes on the Phenomenology of Home," in David Benjamin, ed., *The Home: Words, Interpretations, Meanings and Environments* (Aldershot, U.K.: Avebury, 1995), 131.

11. Vacations were a creation. . . . Cindy S. Aron, *Working at Play: A History of Vacations in the United States* (New York: Oxford University Press, 1999), 5 and 145-147.

12. A house that has. . . . Gaston Bachelard, *The Poetics of Space*, trans. Maria Jolas (Boston, Beacon Press, 1969), 47.

13. I recall reading a. . . . Alexandra Stoddard, *Feeling at Home: Defining Who You Are and How You Want to Live* (New York: William Morrow and Company, 1999), 180.

14. In his book *The*. . . . Bachelard, 67.

15. The notion of rootedness. . . . Tomas Wikström, "The Home and Housing Modernization," in Benjamin, 279.

16. More families are using. . . . Sue Shellenbarger, "Technology Is Helping 'Commuter Families' to Stay in Touch," *The Wall Street Journal*, 14 February 2001, B1.

17. The home is a. . . . Mihaly Csikszentmihalyi and Eugene Rochberg-Halton, *The Meaning of Things: Domestic Symbols and the Self* (Cambridge, U.K.: Cambridge University Press, 1981), 138.

18. "The meanings that keep. . . . Csikszentmihalyi and Rochberg-Halton, 170.

19. In response to a. . . . Phil Walsh, "When Living Becomes an Inconvenience," *NetFuture*, No. 96, 14 October 1999.

20. Communicating with each other. . . . Paul J. J. Pennartz, "The Experience of Atmosphere," in Irene Cieraad, ed., *At Home: An Anthropology of Domestic Space* (Syracuse, NY: Syracuse University Press, 1999), 103.

21. This seems odd to. . . . Jason Fields and Lynne M. Casper, *America's Families and Living Arrangements:* March 2000.

Current Population Reports, p20-527, U.S. Census Bureau, Washington, D.C., 3.

Also, John Wright, ed., *The New York Times Almanac 2001* (New York: Penguin Reference Books, 2000), 282-283.

22. In their study of. . . . Csikszentmihalyi and Rochberg-Halton, 146-158.

23. The headlines are telling. . . . Eleena de Lisser, "Start-Up Attracts Staff With a Ban on Midnight Oil," *The Wall Street Journal,* 23 August 2000, B1. Lisa Guernsey, "Taking the Offensive Against Cell Phones," *The New York Times,* 11 January 2001, G1.

24. Sixty-five percent of. . . . Shannon Quinn and Leslie Cintron, "If Technology Makes Our Lives Easier, Why Are We So Stressed Out?" *The Boston Globe,* 9 September 2000, A15.

25. Jeffrey Lutzner, who runs. . . . Keith H. Hammonds, "Family Values," *Fast Company,* December 2000, 176.

Selected
Bibliography

Ackerman, James S. *The Villa: Form and Ideology of Country Houses.* Princeton, NJ: Princeton University Press, 1990.

Ahrentzen, Sherry. *Blurring Boundaries: Socio-Spatial Consequences of Working at Home.* Milwaukee: Center for Architecture and Urban Planning Research, University of Wisconsin, 1987, reprinted 1990.

_____. *Hybrid Housing: A Contemporary Building Type for Multiple Residential and Business Use.* Milwaukee: Center for Architecture and Urban Planning Research, University of Wisconsin, 1991.

Alderman, Ellen and Caroline Kennedy. *The Right to Privacy.* New York: Alfred A. Knopf, 1995.

Allen, Kathi S. and Gloria Flynn Moorman. "Leaving Home: The Emigration of Home-Office Workers," *American Demographics* 19, no. 10 (October 1997): 57-61.

Aron, Cindy S. *Working at Play: A History of Vacations in the United States.* New York: Oxford University Press, 1999.

Bachelard, Gaston. *The Poetics of Space.* Maria Jolas, trans. N.p.: Press Universitaires de France, 1958; paperback, Boston: Beacon Press, 1969.

Becker, Franklin et al. *The Ecology of the Mobile Worker.* Ithaca, NY: Cornell University International Workplace Studies Program, 1995.

Becker, Penny Edgell and Phyllis Moen. "Scaling Back: Dual-Earner Couples' Work-Family Strategies," *Journal of Marriage and the Family* 61 (November 1999): 995-1007.

Benjamin, David, ed. *The Home: Words, Interpretations, Meanings and Environments.* Aldershot, U.K.: Avebury, 1995.

Buchholz, Ester Schaler. *The Call of Solitude: Alonetime in a World of Attachment.* New York: Simon & Schuster, 1997.

Buder, Stanley. Pullman: *An Experiment in Industrial Order and Community Planning, 1880-1930*. New York: Oxford University Press, 1967.

Busch, Akiko. *Geography of Home: Writings on Where We Live*. New York: Princeton Architectural Press, 1999.

Chaplin, Davina. "Consuming Work/Productive Leisure: The Consumption Patterns of Second Home Environments," *Leisure Studies* 18, no. 1 (1999), 41-55.

Christensen, Kathleen. *Women and Home-Based Work: The Unspoken Contract*. New York: Henry Holt and Company, 1988.

Cieraad, Irene, ed. *At Home: An Anthropology of Domestic Space*. Syracuse, NY: Syracuse University Press, 1999.

Ciulla, Joanne B. *The Working Life: The Promise and Betrayal of Modern Work*. New York: Times Books, 2000.

Clark, Clifford Edward, Jr. *The American Family Home: 1800-1960*. Chapel Hill, NC: The University of North Carolina Press, 1986.

Cohn, Jan. *The Palace or the Poorhouse: The American House as a Cultural Symbol*. East Lansing, MI: The Michigan State University Press, 1979.

Colton, Robert. *Rambles in Sweden and Gottland*. London: Richard Bentley, 1847.

Coontz, Stephanie. *The Social Origins of Private Life: A History of American Families 1600-1900*. London: Verso, 1991.

Crawford, Margaret. *Building the Workingman's Paradise: The Design of American Company Towns*. London: Verso, 1995.

Cross, Amy Willard. *The Summer House: A Tradition of Leisure*. New York: Harper Collins, 1992.

Csikszentmihalyi, Mihaly and Eugene Rochberg-Halton. *The Meaning of Things: Domestic Symbols and the Self*. Cambridge, U.K.: Cambridge University Press, 1981.

Darrah, Charles N., J. A. English-Lueck, and Andrea Saveri. "The Infomated Households Project," *Practicing Anthropology* 19, no. 4 (1997): 18-22.

Dickinson, Duo. *Small Houses for the Next Century*, second edition. New York: McGraw-Hill, Inc., 1995.

Downman, Lorna, Paul Britten Austin, and Anthony Baird. *Round the Swedish Year: Daily Life and Festivals Through Four Seasons.* Stockholm: Bokförlaget Fabel, 1965.

Dyson, Esther. *Release 2.0: A Design for Living in the Digital Age.* New York: Broadway Books, 1997.

Etzioni, Amitai. *The Limits of Privacy.* New York: Basic Books, 1999.

Facos, Michelle. "Definitely Swedish: Carl Larsson's Home in Sundborn," *Scandinavian Review* 81, no. 2 (1993), 62-67.

Fischer, Christiane, ed. *Let Them Speak for Themselves: Women in the American West, 1849-1900,* second edition. Hamden, CT: The Shoe String Press, 1977; Archon Books, imprint of Shoe String, 1990.

Flanagan, Barbara. "The Suburban House Reconsidered," *Metropolis* 117, no. 7 (April 1998), 44.

Galinsky, Ellen. *Ask the Children: What America's Children Really Think About Working Parents.* New York: William Morrow and Company, 1999.

Garber, Marjorie. *Sex and Real Estate: Why We Love Houses.* New York: Pantheon Books, 2000.

Gershenfeld, Neil. *When Things Start to Think.* New York: Henry Holt and Company, 1999.

Gillis, John R. *A World of Their Own Making: Myth, Ritual, and the Quest for Family Values.* New York: Basic Books, 1996.

Hareven, Tamara K. and Randolph Langenbach. *Amoskeag: Life and Work in an American Factory City.* New York: Pantheon Books, 1978.

Hareven, Tamara K. *Family Time and Industrial Time: The Relationship Between the Family and Work in a New England Industrial Community.* Cambridge, England: Cambridge University Press, 1982.

Hayden, Dolores. *Redesigning the American Dream: The Future of Housing, Work, and Family Life.* New York: W.W. Norton and Company, 1984; Norton paperback, 1986.

Hermanuz, Ghislaine. "Outgrowing the Corner of the Kitchen Table," in Joan Rothschild, ed. *Design and*

Feminism: Re-Visioning Spaces, Places, and Everyday Things. New Brunswick, NJ: Rutgers University Press, 1999: 67-83.

James, Henry. "An Autumn Impression" and "The Sense of Newport," in *The American Scene*. New York: Harper and Brothers, 1907; reprint, Bloomington, IN: Indiana University Press, 1968.

Jönsson, Bodil. *Unwinding the Clock: Ten Thoughts on Our Relationship to Time*. Tiina Nunnally, trans. New York: Harcourt, 2001.

Joy, Bill. "Why the Future Doesn't Need Us," *Wired* 8, no. 4 (April 2000): 238.

Junestrand, S. and K. Tollmar. "The Dwelling as a Place for Work," in N. Streitz, S. Konomi, and H. J. Burkhardt, eds. *Cooperative Buildings: Integrating Information, Organization, and Architecture*. Proceedings, Lecture Notes in Computer Science. Heidelberg: Springer, 1998: 230-247.

Klopfer, Peter H. and Daniel I. Rubenstein. "The Concept Privacy and Its Biological Basis," *Journal of Social Issues* 33, no. 3 (1977): 52-65.

Lagerfield, Steven. "Who Knows Where the Time Goes?" *The Wilson Quarterly* 22, no. 3 (Summer 1998), 58-70.

Laufer, Robert S. and Maxine Wolfe. "Privacy as a Concept and a Social Issue: A Multidimensional Developmental Theory," *Journal of Social Issues* 33, no. 3 (1977), 22-42.

Lawrence, Roderick J. "What Makes a House a Home?" *Environment and Behavior* 19, no. 2 (1987), 154-168.

Leyendecker, Liston E. *Palace Car Prince: A Biography of George Mortimer Pullman*. Niwot, CO: University Press of Colorado, 1992.

Löfgren, Orvar. "The Sweetness of Home: Class, Culture and Family Life in Sweden," *Ethnologia Europaea* 14 (1984), 44-64.

_____. "Family and Household Among Scandinavian Peasants: An Exploratory Essay," *Ethnologia Scandinaviea* (1974), 17-52.

Mack, Arien. Home: *A Place in the World*. New York: New York University Press, 1993.

Marc, Olivier. *Psychology of the House*. Jessie Wood, trans. London: Thames and Hudson, 1977.

Marcus, Clare Cooper. *House as a Mirror of Self: Exploring the Deeper Meaning of Home*. Berkeley, CA: Conari Press, 1995.

Margulis, Stephen T., "Conceptions of Privacy: Current Status and Next Steps," *Journal of Social Issues* 33, no. 3 (1977): 5-21.

May, Elaine Tyler. "Myths and Realities of the American Family," in Antoine Prost and Gerard Vincent, eds. *A History of Private Life: Riddles of Identity in Modern Times*. Cambridge, MA: Harvard University Press, Belknap Press, 1991.

Mendelson, Cheryl. *Home Comforts: The Art and Science of Keeping House*. New York: Scribner, 1999.

Michelson, William, Karin Palm Lindén, and Tomas Wikström. "Forward to the Past? Home-Based Work and the Meaning, Use and Design of Residential Space," in S. Kern. *The Culture of Time and Space*. Cambridge, MA: Harvard University Press, 1983: 155-184.

Mitchell, William J. *e-topia: "Urban Life, Jim—But Not as We Know It."* Cambridge, MA: The MIT Press, 1999.

Moen, Phyllis and Yan Yu. "Having It All: Overall Work/Life Success in Two-Earner Families," *Research in the Sociology of Work*. Volume 7. Greenwich, CT: JAI Press, 1999: 109-139.

Moen, Phyllis with Deborah Harris-Abbott, Shinok Lee, and Patricia Roehling. "The Cornell Couples and Careers Study." Ithaca, NY: Cornell Employment and Family Careers Institute, 1999.

Montgomery, David. *Citizen Worker: The Experience of Workers in the United States with Democracy and the Free Market during the Nineteenth Century*. Cambridge, England: Cambridge University Press, 1993.

Moore-Ede, Martin. *The Twenty-Four Hour Society*. Reading, MA: Addison-Wesley Publishing Co., 1993.

Naisbitt, John with Nana Naisbitt and Douglas Philips. *High Tech, High Touch: Technology and Our Search for Meaning.* New York: Broadway Books, 1999.

Nippert-Eng, Christena E. *Home and Work: Negotiating Boundaries Through Everyday Life.* Chicago: The University of Chicago Press, 1995; paperback, University of Chicago Press, 1996.

Ogburn, William F. "Technology as Environment," in Ogburn, *On Culture and Social Change: Selected Papers.* Chicago: The University of Chicago Press, 1964.

Owen, David. *Around the House: Reflections on Life Under a Roof.* New York: Villard, 1998.

Pahl, Ray. *After Success: Fin de Siecle Anxiety and Identity.* Cambridge, UK: Polity Press, 1995.

Pipher, Mary. *The Shelter of Each Other: Rebuilding Our Families.* New York: G.P. Putnam's Sons, 1996.

Popenoe, David. *Disturbing the Nest: Family Change and Decline in Modern Societies.* New York: Aldine de Gruyter, 1988.

Riley, Terence. *The Un-Private House.* New York: The Museum of Modern Art, 1999.

Robinson, John P. and Geoffrey Godbey. *Time for Life: The Surprising Ways Americans Use Their Time*, second edition. University Park, PA: The Pennsylvania State University Press, 1999.

Rosen, Jeffrey. *The Unwanted Gaze: The Destruction of Privacy in America.* New YorkL Random House, 2000.

Rybczynski, Witold. "The Biggest Small Buildings," *Architecture 87*, no. 12 (December 1998), 56-59.

_____. *Home: A Short History of an Idea.* New York: Viking Penguin, 1986; paperback, New York: Penguin Books, 1987.

_____. *Looking Around: A Journey Through Architecture.* New York: Viking Penguin, 1992.

_____. *Waiting for the Weekend.* New York: Viking Penguin, 1991.

Rydin, Lena. *Carl Larsson-gården: A Home.* Malung, Sweden: Carl Larsson-garden/Dalaförlaget, 1994.

Shapiro, Stuart. "Places and Spaces: The Historical Interaction of Technology, Home and Privacy," *The Information Society* 14 (1998), 275-284.

Silverstone, Roger and Eric Hirsch, eds. *Consuming Technologies: Media and Information in Domestic Spaces.* London: Routledge, 1992.

Smith, Janna Malamud. *Private Matters: In Defense of the Personal Life.* Reading, MA: Addison-Wesley, 1997.

Sopher, David E. "The Landscape of Home: Myth, Experience, Social Meaning" in D. W. Meinig, ed. *The Interpretation of Ordinary Landscapes: Geographical Essays.* New York: Oxford University Press, 1979.

Stage, Sarah and Virginia B. Vincenti, eds. *Rethinking Home Economics: Women and the History of a Profession.* Ithaca, NY: Cornell University Press, 1997

Stoddard, Alexandra. *Feeling at Home: Defining Who You Are and How You Want to Live.* New York: William Morrow & Company, 1999.

Strasser, Susan. *Never Done: A History of American Housework.* New York: Pantheon Books, 1982.

von Heidenstam, Oscar Gustaf. *Swedish Life in Town and Country.* New York: G.P. Putnam's Sons, The Knickerbocker Press, 1904.

Ware, Norman. *The Industrial Worker, 1840-1860: The Reaction of American Industrial Society to the Advance of the Industrial Revolution.* Boston: Houghton Mifflin, 1924; reprinted, Chicago: Elephant Paperbacks, 1990.

Weil, Michelle M. and Larry D. Rosen. *TechnoStress: Coping with Technology @ Work, @ Home, @ Play.* New York: John Wiley & Sons, 1997

Westerberg, Ulla. "Dwelling Habits and Values—Inertia and Change in Sweden," in J. Teklenburg et al. *Shifting Balances, Changing Roles in Policy, Research and Design, Proceedings of the 15th Bi-Annual Conference of the International Association for People-Environment Studies.* European Institute of Retailing and Service Studies, 1998.

White, E. B. "Once More to the Lake," in *One Man's Meat*. New York: Harper & Brothers, 1938, 1944.

Wikström, Tomas, William Michelson, and Karin Palm Lindén. *Hub of Events or Splendid Isolation: The Home as a Context for Teleworking*. Stockholm: KFB, 1998.

Wilson, Peter J. *The Domestication of the Human Species*. New Haven, CT: Yale University Press, 1988.

Wolfe, Alan. *One Nation, After All*. New York: Viking Penguin, 1998.

MAGGIE JACKSON, the national workplace columnist for The Associated Press since 1994, and a contributor to National Public Radio, *The New York Times* and other publications, reports on issues from corporate daycare to harassment to office romance. Jackson received a B.A. in English from Yale University in 1982 and a degree in International Politics from the London School of Economics in 1990. She also served as a foreign desk editor and business desk editor at The Associated Press. Jackson was the recipient of an Alfred P. Sloan Foundation grant to research and report on Centers on Working Families across the country. In 2001, she was honored with the 3rd Annual Conference Board/Families and Work Institute Award for Outstanding Work-Life Journalism, and has received several Front Page awards from the Newswomen's Club of New York. Jackson lives in New York City with her husband and children.